MARCI ALBORGHETTI

WHEN LIGHTNING STRIKES TWICE

TWENTY-THIRD PUBLICATIONS

185 WILLOW STREET • PO BOX 180 • MYSTIC, CT 06355
TEL: 1-800-321-0411 • FAX: 1-800-572-0788
E-MAIL: ttpubs@aol.com • www.twentythirdpublications.com

Twenty percent of the royalties from this book will be donated to the Mothers' Union Sierra Leone Preschool project in Freetown, Sierra Leone. For more information, please feel free to contact me at **inklin@ntplx.net**

—*Marci Alborghetti*

Twenty-Third Publications
A Division of Bayard
185 Willow Street
P.O. Box 180
Mystic, CT 06355
(860) 536-2611 or (800) 321-0411
www.twentythirdpublications.com
ISBN:1-58595-378-4

Library of Congress Catalog Card Number: 2004109203
Printed in the U.S.A.

DEDICATION

For God.
To Charlie.
As always.

ACKNOWLEDGMENTS

In writing this, I have tried to be faithful to the gifts and vision God has given me. I am grateful for every blessing. This book, perhaps more than any other of mine, required a great deal of human help as well. I am usually astonished and often skeptical when an author waxes eloquent about his or her publisher. Not any more. My publisher, Gwen Costello, quite literally resurrected this manuscript, giving its author the hope and encouragement that is reflected in every page. I can't thank her enough. My editor, Mary Carol Kendzia, has once again made me seem more literate than I am. The rest of the staff at Twenty-Third Publications/Bayard has been wonderful, including me in all that great and mysterious stuff that happens after the manuscript is completed.

Those who contributed immeasurably to this book and who have my most heartfelt appreciation include the unwaveringly supportive members of my group, especially Betty, Joe, and Rita; also Lisa Giordano; Ruby Watrous; and Joni Woelfel.

I must thank my family and friends who struggle to give me the gift of solitude; I know it is not easy.

Finally, in the tradition of the last shall be first, I cannot express my gratitude and love for Charlie Duffy, my primary proofreader and constant champion.

CONTENTS

INTRODUCTION

Surviving devastating events like the death of a loved one, illness, natural disaster, accident, addiction, or divorce is extremely difficult. Surviving the same or similar event the second time around can seem all but impossible. Yet many people find themselves in just this situation: tragedy strikes again in their lives.

When my doctor found a new melanoma after I'd been officially "clean" for six years, I was stunned. When in the ensuing process of multiple biopsies, he found the beginning of another one, I was devastated. Everything I thought I'd learned the first time around seemed to escape my grasp. It was like starting over with the original diagnosis. Except worse. When God blessed me with more healing, it took a while for my mind and spirit to catch up with my body. Eventually, I realized I was not alone; that "second strikes" come in every shape, size, and form, and that they can be brutally hard to survive.

Perhaps surprisingly to those who haven't faced such a "second strike," the experience is often much more difficult the second time around. While it may seem as though it should be easier—after all, it can be argued, you've been through it once, so it should be "familiar territory" and easier to negotiate—many who live through repeat tragedies find it to be just the opposite. We feel more shocked, more debilitated, simply because we believed that this nightmare was behind us. We thought we'd addressed it and moved on, so the sudden, stunning return is even more crushing.

For people who have worked hard to overcome an addiction, become a better spouse, or adopt a healthy, positive lifestyle, a new addiction, a second troubled marriage and even divorce, or a second descent into illness can also represent personal failure. This sharp sense of shortcoming merely adds to the burden of the "second strike." Quite often it takes longer to "power up," or gird ourselves to deal with the issue when it levels us again.

Even more disturbing to those of us facing a repeated crisis is the initial impact it may have on our faith and relationship with God. In many cases we'd managed to overcome—or at least weather—the first storm by calling upon faith and drawing closer to God. A greater faith and a deeper intimacy with God could well have resulted from the first experience. Over time we may have also come to believe, sometimes subconsciously, that God intended to protect us forever from a recurrence. So when we find ourselves facing the very thing that we've counted on God to prevent, we can feel betrayed. This feeling of betrayal or even abandonment can send victims of a "second strike" into a spiritual tailspin, leading to guilt over such doubts and feelings of spiritual loss or inadequacy.

These pages will explore all of these feelings and examine how people in the grip of repeat tragedy experience the event, face their circumstances, learn to cope, and find their way to a stronger faith and deeper trust in God. Using life stories, anecdotes, biblical profiles, and illustrations from our culture, each chapter will define and describe a stage or emotion in the experience of a second tragedy. The chapters will progress toward self-examination, deeper faith and resolution. At the end of each chapter will be a prayer conversation with God, questions for reflection, suggested from the Bible readings, and activities designed to assist in dealing with a return tragedy. Finally, this book is written in the spirit of hope and the abiding certainty that God accompanies our every step.

CHAPTER ONE

DISBELIEF:
IT CAN'T BE!

No, my daughters, it has been far more bitter for me than for you, because the hand of the Lord has turned against me.   Ruth 1:13

Naomi and her family had been driven into a strange land where, after struggling and working hard to make a completely new start, after becoming moderately successful even as exiles, everything fell apart. Her husband died. Her first son died. Her second son died. She was alone, with no visible means of income, left with two foreign daughters-in-law to support.

Tragedy after tragedy struck the family until Naomi, the driving force in the Old Testament's Book of Ruth, came to believe that God had turned against her. Naomi was unquestionably a woman of great faith, and yet her spirit was bowed under renewed anguish. Her cry is all the more poignant because of her deep faith. And just as Jesus expressed in his cry on the cross, Naomi finds herself wondering why God has seemingly forsaken her.

That's how recurring tragedy can feel, and while some people, mercifully, cannot fathom Naomi's disbelief and gripping sorrow, Kathryn can. When she married she left Savannah, the warm, southern city where she was born and raised, to follow her new husband, Vic, to the cold, inhospitable coast of Maine. They settled into a rickety old cottage, and he began to work long hours at the job that had lured him north. Often she was lonely, and in the early days, tight finances kept her from returning home to her big southern family more than once each year. However much she loved Vic, she still craved the affection of her family and friends, not to mention the slow, friendly Dixie lifestyle she was accustomed to.

She particularly dreaded the seemingly endless, cold Maine winters, and she found her neighbors and the wives of Vic's colleagues strangely aloof. To make matters worse, their rambling cottage was on a slender peninsula, and during storms they were sometimes cut off from town by flooding or ice. It happened twice in their first winter, and both times Kathryn was left alone in the cottage because Vic couldn't get back from work. She recalls shivering under a pile of blankets and afghans, listening to the pitiless northeast wind and wondering why she'd ever left her mother's house.

Still, Vic and Kathryn had planned to start a family, one of the reasons they'd decided she would not work, and soon the children came. There were three in all, and with each new birth, Kathryn found herself growing more content in her new home. "I felt like all those times when I had nothing to depend on but my faith and God had finally paid off. The kids became my whole life, and I truly felt they were a gift from God." Time passed more quickly than she could have imagined. Before she thought it possible, her oldest boy was married with a daughter of his own, and her youngest son was a freshman at Boston University, the same college from which his older sister would soon graduate. It was during this golden, joyous time of life, that the dream-finally-come-true became a nightmare.

Shortly before their daughter graduated during an unseasonably warm May, Kathryn and Vic were awakened after midnight on a

Saturday. Their town had a very small police department, and when Kathryn saw the chief at the door, she says, "I felt my heart drop, almost like a lead weight, into my stomach. I knew even as my mind desperately rejected knowing." The officer told them that their oldest son had fallen asleep behind the wheel of his truck and crashed into a telephone pole. Kathryn found herself unable to grasp what had happened.

"Even though I saw the look on his face, I heard myself asking, 'Is he all right?' I just couldn't make myself believe what I already knew was true."

In a haze of denial and inexpressible grief, Vic and Kathryn buried their eldest son the week before their daughter graduated. "Looking back, I feel terrible about that," Kathryn recalls. "She graduated with honors from a very difficult program, and we hardly noticed."

Before the grieving process could truly begin, "before I could really begin to pray again," the long years of long hours at a stressful job took their toll in a matter of seconds. When the same police chief came to Kathryn's door late one sunny September day, she felt she was plummeting into an abyss. She remembers, "My mind started to scream one word: Vic! But I immediately shut it down. The idea that he, too, had been in an accident—probably coming home from work—was just impossible for me. I was so determined to reject it that I think I even had a smile on my face when I opened the door. Can you believe that?!"

Vic, it turned out, hadn't been in an accident. He'd collapsed at work, the victim of a massive heart attack. Kathryn and her daughter made it to the hospital in time to say good-bye, though Vic never regained consciousness. Their youngest son was too far away, at BU, to make it home before his father died.

For the second time in four months, Kathryn stood at the tiny wind-swept cemetery, dry-eyed. "Everyone else was crying," she remembers, "The neighbors and co-workers I'd thought so cold almost thirty years ago were sobbing out loud. My kids were a mess. My daughter-in-law had to take my little granddaughter back to the house because she was wailing so wrenchingly. But I didn't cry. It never occurred to me. And I wasn't able to help any of them, even though I felt I should. I just didn't believe all this had happened. It was like it was happening to someone else. I think I refused to believe it, because I feared that if I really let it sink in, I would lose touch with the one comfort I'd always had: God. As much as I didn't want to admit it, I was wondering why God had let these horrible things happen to me, and I just didn't want to ask that question aloud. I was afraid."

Kathryn remained in denial through the next months. Even when the weather turned bad and the access road to her house was flooded and then frozen, she refused to heed her children's pleas to consider moving. "My daughter had an apartment in Portland where she was working, and she begged me to come live with her. She told me we didn't have to sell the house right away, that I should just leave it for the winter season, but I didn't listen. I couldn't. This was our home. I think I felt that if I stayed, maybe everything would be the way it was. So I did, even as the road flooded and the cellar filled with water…and then that froze!" Kathryn smiles at herself now, but then she felt only that she'd finally become as cold as her adopted home.

By spring, Kathryn's lifelong faith had begun to do its thawing work. When the numbness finally receded, she underwent many excruciating days, weeks, and even months before she learned to pour her anguish out to God without necessarily expecting an answer or resolution. "You come to a place," she explains softly, "where, if you are going to choose faith, you need to acknowledge that God has all the cards, and you only get a glimpse at the end of every hand. There's an acceptance that comes with that. But it wasn't easy at first. I couldn't feel anything. And then for awhile, I felt uncertain about my bond with God, about whether he still loved me."

Many people, confronted with extreme or repeated loss, have the same experience of instant, numbing disbelief and confusion about God and faith. In many ways such a "shut-down" response is truly a gift from a loving God who understands that we simply can't absorb so much pain all at once. Many therapists and mental health professionals suggest that it is a very human defense mechanism that kicks in to protect the psyche and sanity of the victim. There's no reason to think that the two theories are not compatible since God created us to be wonderfully and exquisitely adaptable.

So it is likely that the Creator gifted us with an ability to freeze out emotions and even events that threaten to destroy our faith, sanity, and, perhaps, our lives. This gift is what allows people to continue to function, at least superficially, after a death. They plan the funeral, order the flowers, arrange for the readings, call the relatives, all in a seemingly calm, methodical way while feeling the whole time, as Kathryn observed, that everything is happening to someone else. There are some things in life that are simply too massive to immediately comprehend and address; God understands this. Indeed, there is some pain so excruciating that our Lord may keep it at a distance from us for all our lives here on earth.

In the first season of the popular TV series, *The West Wing*, there is a scene set during the Christmas season wherein Mrs. Landingham, the indefatigable secretary to the president, is having a conversation with Charlie, the president's personal assistant. Charlie observes that Mrs. Landingham doesn't seem particularly enthusiastic about the Christmas season. She pauses at her desk, but barely stops working as she explains, in a very matter-of-fact monotone, that she lost both her sons during the Christmas season years ago in Vietnam.

Charlie, stunned by the shockingly bland revelation, asks why her sons didn't seek deferments since they were both in medical school and could have easily ducked the draft. They were not drafted, she replied, they volunteered, probably because she and her husband had raised them to respect and serve their country. Charlie, dumbfounded and unable to fashion a response, starts to turn away when Mrs. Landingham says in the same monotone that she often wonders what her sons' last minutes were like. It seems to me, she says, that they might have really wanted their mother in those moments as they lay frightened and dying. And then she returns to her computer screen.

Of course, their mother was not there, and viewers of this memorable scene are left to understand that all these years later, their mother has never quite been able to absorb the anguish of that fact.

God created individuals, enabling each of us to react as we need to. The disbelieving response to agony may be expressed "loud and clear" as well as through insensate disbelief. In many cultures, dramatic expressions of rending grief are considered necessary for the mourners, especially the family members, to be able to fully experience and recognize their loss and eventually move on. These displays are also thought to be a vital demonstration of respect for the dead.

In the West African nation of Sierra Leone, among other African countries, it is expected that neighbors, colleagues, and friends will greet a family or individual in mourning with a tremendous show of grief for their loss. There will be copious tears, wailing, and even falling to the ground to recognize the loss of the loved one. Even the sight of a son, daughter, or other relative who closely resembles the deceased can provoke such a moving display. A Sierra Leone native says that this form of extravagant mourning is a sign of respect for the person who died and empathy for the family members.

"It is the customary way for our people to show how much the person meant to them, and even more, to his family," explains Sylvia, who divides her time between the United States and her homeland. "In a way, you could say it is how we celebrate the person's life and show the living how much we sympathize with their great loss." Family, friends, colleagues, and acquaintances also plan and attend lengthy and often beautiful ceremonies after death and at selected anniversaries. There are myriad native dishes and extended periods of prescribed mourning, all to remember the dead with as much joy as grief.

People who rail and keen against personal tragedy are giving honest and full voice to their despair and sense of loss. This, too, is a common and sincere response, though many of us may prefer to see the dry-eyed, frozen-hearted widow rather than the distraught, hysterical mourner who cannot bear to let the casket be lowered into the ground. We may be more comfortable with the first response, and even consider it more "seemly," most likely because it does not force us to consider the inevitability that we, too, may some day experience such grief; nor does it require anything of us beyond a few muttered words.

But our empathetic God does not discriminate against us because of how we respond to searing tragedy. The ultimate loving parent accepts each person's grief, confusion, and even denial, regardless of how it is expressed. The Lord understands, and does not require us to present a pre-formed facade. God knows how we will react before we know how we will react. Indeed God knows how we will react before the event even occurs. If we need to wrap ourselves in the protection of frozen numbness, God understands. If we need to honor and celebrate a life, God understands. If we need to wail and rail, God understands. God has made us the way we are, and therefore will not be surprised, much less disturbed, by anything we do in the face of repeated disaster. Even if we feel against all our hope and rational belief, as Naomi did, that the hand of the Lord has turned against us, God understands and forgives us.

And then, God merely waits.

TALKING IT OVER WITH GOD

Father, I am utterly overwhelmed by sorrow and confusion. I cannot believe what has happened in my life. Again. I cannot face it. I cannot deal with the anguish and the fear. And I am terrified by the questions lurking just behind my disbelief. How could you have let this happen to me, Lord? Would this have happened if you really loved me? Haven't I been through enough? Haven't I stayed true to you through much pain? What am I supposed to do now? What do you expect of me? What can I expect of you?

Lord, I fear that my faith will not be strong enough to weather this. Please help me. Help me to turn to you again with my broken, damaged heart. Help me to confront this when I am ready, and help me to know that you are still by my side. I feel so helpless, Lord! I feel so hopeless! I am like a lost, frightened child waiting for someone to take my hand and lead me out of this nightmarish maze. Uncurl my fingers from the tight, closed fist I've formed and hold my hand firmly in yours, Lord. Lead me to the people, the places, the prayers that will bring me back to life. Lead me back to you, Lord.

ASK YOURSELF

1. Have you ever been stunned to the point of disbelief by the recurrence of an event, illness, or circumstance that you thought was in your past?

2. Do you believe it's more difficult to move through the initial stage of a tragedy when it happens a second time?

3. Can you think of ways to avoid despair after learning that a tragedy has recurred in your life?

Taking Further Action

• Rent the movie *Sophie's Choice* and focus on how Meryl Streep's character was affected, first by war and then by the devastating choice forced on her by that war.

• Read the story of Naomi in the Book of Ruth, chapters 1—2.

• Go to a quiet place where you've been able to pray or meditate in the past. Sit in a comfortable chair or position. Breathe deeply and slowly. Imagine your heartbeat becoming slow and regular. Direct your thoughts to the first time this event or illness struck your life. Remember what techniques, prayers, and support systems you used successfully to move beyond the initial stage of disbelief. Recall the ways in which you turned to God. Consider how these might work in the present situation. Resolve to implement the ones most likely to aid you now.

CHAPTER TWO

SHOCK

Be gracious to me, O Lord, for I am languishing; O Lord, heal me, for my bones are shaking with terror. My soul also is struck with terror, while you, O Lord—how long?　　　　　Psalm 6:2–3

King David, though beloved, advanced, and protected by Yahweh, penned many psalms that express his uncertainty about God's presence. Despite David's position as one specifically chosen by God, shock and fearful confusion about the troubles in his life are frequent themes in his writing.

Five years ago when Joe tripped on an poorly-placed pipe behind the bar in the upscale restaurant where he worked, he really didn't feel shock, confusion, or fear. Indeed, he thought it was nothing more than an unfortunate work-related accident that would have no lasting effect or greater consequence than to keep him out of work for a few days.

Today Joe is the living definition of shock, confusion, and fear, not to mention agonizing pain. After an initial trip to the emergency room for a possible head injury, Joe was sent home and told to take it easy for a few days. He waited restlessly for the few days to pass and returned to work as soon as he could. After all, he'd spent twenty years using his affable nature and professional skills to build a successful career in the food and beverage service industry. He'd traveled in pursuit of what became his vocation and avocation, working in popular cities like San Francisco, Newport, and Key West. He'd served the rich and famous as well as the poor and hard-working with equal aplomb.

"I loved my job, and I was good at it," Joe now recounts. "I took real satisfaction in making people happy and in having a top-notch reputation in the service industry. I enjoyed every minute of my life."

That's why the multiple strikes Joe has experienced over the past five years since the accident have been so devastating: not only did his accident result, first, in the loss of his job; second, in the loss of a lifelong career; and third, in the loss of his lifestyle and self-esteem, it brought on excruciating cluster headaches which para-lyzed him with pain and nausea just about every day. He literally lost the life he'd known.

"Shortly after I returned to work, I knew something was wrong. I wasn't at the top of my game like usual. I couldn't remember every-thing I was supposed to do. I couldn't serve my customers they way I used to," Joe says. "Eventually, I went to part-time, but even that didn't work. The headaches started. I couldn't work. I began to be afraid of leaving the house in case one of the clusters struck while I was out. Within a very short time I went from being one of the most outgoing guys in the world to being a virtual shut-in."

Now in his forties, Joe was forced to move into the home of his older sister, Rita, who became his caretaker while also juggling her own full-time job. She grimly watched his life unravel before her eyes, and her own anguish as she saw him reel under the burden of sorrow after sorrow nearly matched his.

"Everything went wrong, one thing after another," Rita says. "First it was the accident, then the job loss, then the unexpected, unimaginable pain, then doctor after doctor after doctor saying they couldn't figure out how to treat him. It was horrible. Add to that the constant confusion with the employer over who should pay for what. And then there were the court depositions. It was like each new shot just drained the life out of him. He started feeling paranoid. We both started feeling paranoid! There were times when we were just basket cases."

Joe spent a lot of time in shock. Even today he will repeat softly, as though he still can't believe it, "I had everything I wanted...and then it was all gone."

Blind with pain, stunned by what had happened to him, Joe finally reached out for the one thing he had left: his faith. Rita's house was near the church and parochial school that he had attended as a child. By the time Joe accepted that God was all he had left, he was practically a self-incarcerated prisoner in his sister's home. He didn't dare leave the house, fearful that he might have an attack and worried that people he might meet would notice how debilitated he'd become.

"I was afraid. And embarrassed," he declares bluntly. "Besides the pain, I was so emotionally destroyed by what had happened to me. It had changed me so much, I'd lost my ability to socialize. I was afraid that people who'd known the old me would be appalled by how different I was. So I avoided going out. And when I tried to force myself, I often couldn't make it to the door of where I intended to go...that is, if I'd managed to force myself out of our door to even get that far! By the time I understood that God wanted me to go to morning Mass, all I could do at first was drive myself a few blocks to the church and stare at the door. Some days I couldn't even get out of the car."

Eventually, with the help of Rita and an extraordinarily sensitive pastor, Joe made it through the church door. The pastor let Joe move at his own pace, and on the few occasions when he wanted to talk, the priest listened. Soon they were regularly exchanging at least a few words. Perceiving that Joe might be ready for the next step, the pastor asked him whether he'd occasionally like to serve at morning Mass.

A former altar boy, Joe knew what to do, he just wasn't sure he could do it. He was afraid of disappointing the priest who'd been so supportive. But he also felt that God was calling him to take this next step, and the connection with his childhood—a simpler, clearer time—was vivid for Joe. "What I'd had at this church, growing up, well, those good things were all still there for me," he observes. "At my church, it didn't matter that I'd been at the top of my world and then lost everything. I had a chance to start again where I'd originally begun my life."

Joe continued to be crippled nearly every night by the cluster headaches, but he forced himself to take small steps during the day. Refusing to lose hope, he and Rita continued to explore increasingly elusive treatment options, and they joined a support group held in the basement of a local public library. There, they found themselves able to share their story with others who were also struggling with a variety of painful issues. The relief they both felt at finding an opportunity to simply be honest and accepted, was welcome.

Meanwhile, Joe's pastor saw another opportunity. Learning that Joe had been a much sought after professional in the restaurant world, and knowing that Rita herself was no slouch in the kitchen, the priest asked them to cater a small party—for the bishop! Forcing back the panic that initially flooded every fiber of his mind and body, Joe focused on his faith, talked it over with Rita, and agreed to take the job. When he and Rita made the announcement to their support group, a cheer went up that made the library patrons upstairs wonder just what kind of meeting was being held. Joe, with the approval of his sister and group, made a plan, designed a menu, and established a strict cooking and serving timetable that would keep the bishop on schedule for the rest of the evening.

For the first time in nearly five years, he was doing his job.

The dinner was superb and led to more catering opportunities within the large parish. Rita, delighted to see her brother embracing such a challenge, was a willing participant in the venture. The horrible shock that had accompanied Joe's many losses gradually became a sense of wonderment at the small gifts that had come his way. "Despite the almost daily pain, I am so thankful. I know God has brought these people into my life, and I know I'm moving in a healthier direction," says Joe, who also credits his therapist for encouraging him in his progress. "True, I'm still waiting for resolution on a number of issues, but I feel like God has given me a chance to get my life back."

Like King David, both Joe and Rita know what it is to be besieged by sorrow, betrayal, pain, and loss. And like the Old Testament's most celebrated monarch, they turned to God in their shock and grief. Christian writer Marion Bond West suggests this is the only option available to people who have absorbed so many blows, they have been forced to the edge of an abyss.

In her book, *The Nevertheless Principle*, West describes her own journey from paralyzing despair when cancer returns to reclaim the life of her husband, to unquestioning faith. In the first pages of the book, she makes it clear to her readers and to God that her greatest fear in life was the loss of her husband. She had four children when he first became ill, with twin boys still at home, and she painfully details her terror at the very thought of trying to continue her life alone. She literally cannot imagine doing so, and she initially wears herself out petitioning God, even resorting to bargaining for the life of her husband.

West writes about a revelation she was given when she was finally so exhausted with shock and fear that she had come to the end of her ability to cope alone. "I knew what I looked like on the inside— a city after a hydrogen bomb hit, everything dead and gray and covered in ashes. Nothing moved. No life was ever expected again," she explains in the preface to *The Nevertheless Principle*. "And then in that hopeless desolation...a small green shoot emerged. It was new and tender and only one word tall. Nevertheless. Swiftly it took root in my mind until a sentence appeared: God is not a God of what-if; he is the God of nevertheless."

After researching the many uses of the word nevertheless in the Bible, West discovered that, "nevertheless was no ordinary lifestyle. It was a supernatural way to live, no matter what life dished out—a power and dimension that seemed to be reserved mainly for the desperate. I qualified!" The simple and yet incredibly powerful gift that West describes—the abiding belief that God is with us most powerfully when we most desperately need him—allowed her to face her future with a calm, and even joyful demeanor.

Certainly not everyone can instantly achieve such unalterable faith. Indeed, some of the best known figures in the world of faith have described excruciating feelings of doubt, fear, and paralysis. St. John of the Cross is as well-known for depicting his own disturbing "dark nights of the soul" as he is for his spirituality. More recently revealed, and perhaps more relevantly to those of us who suffer such doubt and confusion today, are astonishing details about how Mother Teresa, renowned for her dauntless work among the poorest and sickest people of the world, was plagued by extended periods of uncertainty about God's presence in her life.

Shortly after her death the church released reports that this internationally recognized figure of mercy, famous for her unfailingly cheerful and pragmatic attitude, lived through months and years when she felt little but the heart-crushing absence of God. For those who followed the career of this selfless woman, whom many considered a living saint and who is, in fact, in the process of being canonized, this was shocking stuff. How could she have continued working in such abject poverty, illness, and filth without the consolation and encouragement of God's constant presence? How could she have become the embodiment of Christianity if she felt that God had abandoned her?

And most disconcerting to us mere mortals, if Mother Teresa couldn't feel God's presence, what chance do the rest of us have?!

Perhaps instead of being astonished and discouraged by Mother Teresa's doubts, those of us struggling with their own pain and sorrow should feel comforted. If this woman, revered throughout the world for her dedication and faith, could continue to believe in God's goodness and ultimate guidance even when she'd lost a sense of God's actual presence, then is she not an even more perfect model for the rest of us? If she could proceed so confidently in the brutal, crushing circumstances of her daily toil and chosen life, in spite of her confusion and occasional uncertainty, then should we not put our heads down, lift our hearts up, and plunge forward?

This is a tenet of faith: from those who have been given much, much will be required. It is a tenet that is open to many interpretations, but the one that most applies to people burdened by tragedy and pain is deceptively simple: the heavier the load we are given, the more we are required to act as people who are able to bear the weight. In other words, just when it may be hardest to feel faithful, we are most compelled to act faithfully.

Joe has a more direct way of expressing this. Reporting that he'd recently been appointed to oversee a weekend-long food event for his parish, he observes, "I'm excited. I'm also scared. Very scared. But I've been feeling nothing—being nothing—for too long, and I'd rather feel scared and excited than feel nothing. I have to believe that God is guiding me; I *do* believe that God is guiding me, and I'm going to let myself be guided."

TALKING IT OVER WITH GOD

Lord, I have felt numb with shock and sorrow for so long. I am also confused. How do I move myself from this place of paralysis and inaction? How can I get beyond the fact that this burden has come back into my life? How can I begin to know how to shoulder it once again? I don't want to! I'm tired. I want to be left alone. I want to sleep. I want to pretend this is not happening again.

But I can't, Lord. I know I can't stay immobile. I know I must allow myself to be guided by you. I know I must actively seek to renew my faith in your presence even when I don't feel up to such a challenge. Teach me how, Lord. Teach me to stop struggling against my circumstance and to relax into your embrace. I am like the small, weak player in a child's game who stands in front of the larger, stronger player. And like that small, weak player, unable to see the one who will catch her, I must trust enough to fall backwards into your strong, waiting arms.

Help me to remember, Lord, that if I trust, you will never let me fall.

ASK YOURSELF

1. Have you ever used shock as a crutch to avoid taking action?

2. In the case of a "second strike," must shock always, even if only briefly, lead to despair?

3. What are the advantages and disadvantages of having someone close to you share the burden of a repeated tragedy?

Taking Further Action

- Read Marion Bond West's book, *The Nevertheless Principle*.
- Read the Psalms of David, focusing on those that reveal a shocked and despairing writer.
- The shock that often accompanies recurring anguish can be paralyzing. To counteract this effect and begin to move toward healing, turn to someone who helped you through the first painful event. This may be a trusted sibling, friend, fellow parishioner, or professional like a nurse or therapist. Put aside shock, reticence, shame, and any emotion which keeps you from examining the facts of your current difficulty. Then describe this situation, using precise details as you perceive them, to this person.

Ask your companion to merely listen at first. If necessary, act as though you are describing someone else's tragedy. Force yourself to be as objective and logical as possible. Start at the beginning and proceed through your present circumstances as though you were providing a report. Get it all out—every detail. If you wish at this point, ask your trusted listener to remind you of ways in which you coped in the past and to suggest ways to address this new challenge.

CHAPTER THREE

RAGE

When Esau heard his father's words, he cried out with an exceed-
ingly great and bitter cry, and said to his father...."Jacob, my broth-
er, has supplanted me these two times. He took away my birthright;
and look, now he has taken away my blessing." Genesis 27:34, 36

Esau provides a clear example of how quickly shock can turn to
rage. Upon learning that his brother had tricked him out of both
his birthright and his father's blessing, Esau becomes infuriated.
His grief and anger know no bounds, and soon he is plotting to
console himself by murdering his brother. Engaging in such violence can do nothing to further his cause and might actually cut
him off from his failing father, but at first he simply does not care.
He is determined to do something, anything, to relieve his rage and
disappointment.

Susan and Jeffrey know what it feels like to have the initial shock
at a recurrent crisis be rapidly replaced by helpless fury. As state
employees, they both benefited from the economic boon of the
mid- and late-nineties. During that happy period, their union
managed to negotiate generous increases in benefits and wages. The
economy was good, so the governor and legislature responded gen-

erously. Susan and Jeffrey bought a new home and enrolled their two children in a private parochial school. Life, as Jeffrey notes with a wry smile, was good.

They didn't pay too much attention when the economy started to go south. After all, they worked for the state government; they had pensions and benefits. Susan admits, "We even felt a little sorry for people who worked for big corporations that were downsizing. We were grateful that we didn't have to worry about keeping stockholders happy."

What they didn't count on was having to keep state residents, themselves feeling the pinch of rising taxes and falling or vanishing incomes, happy. Things seemed to change overnight. With growing trepidation, Susan and Jeffrey read letters to the editor in newspapers from residents demanding that state employees give back wages and benefits or accept layoffs. As the state's budget deficit ballooned, political leaders responded swiftly to their constituents' clamoring demands for lower taxes and more budget cuts. Union leaders refused to budge, preferring to stir up members rather than compromise. Angry skirmishes raged in the legislature for months, but sooner than they might have expected, state employees found themselves facing layoffs. Susan's department was one of the first targeted.

Susan and Jeffrey were disheartened and afraid when Susan got her pink slip. But they didn't panic. They could tighten things up at home, cancel the annual vacation, and if worse came to worse, put their kids back into the public school system. "I guess by then, we were sort of prepared for it," Jeffrey recalls. "She hadn't been working as long as I had because she'd stayed home when the kids were babies. In her department it was sort of a last-hired, first-fired thing, so we weren't blindsided by it. And to be honest, we weren't really angry. If anything we were confused and upset by the fact that so many average people—including our friends and neighbors, I imagine—had turned against state workers with such a vengeance. Hearing and reading people claim we had these wonderful easy jobs, that we were all lazy and had an 'entitlement mentality' because we worked for the government—that hurt."

Anger joined the hurt two months later when Jeffrey lost his job. "We couldn't believe it," Susan says, distress at that memory evident in her voice. "We felt like, 'How could they do this to us? Didn't they understand that both of us worked for the state? And that I'd already been laid off?! We were really caught by surprise because we thought we'd be safe after my layoff. Couldn't they have let at least one of us keep our job so we could support our family?' I felt betrayed by the state. I felt betrayed by our union for not accepting a deal that might have let Jeff keep his job. I didn't care that it was the state and not some big corporation. In fact, I felt that the state—as an employer—had a greater obligation to its employees. I was just furious."

Jeffrey's emotions were more complex. "I guess I felt angry like Susan," he explains, "but my feelings were more of a jumble of bad stuff. Probably because deep down inside I still considered myself the head of the family, the protector. So I felt guilty, as if it was somehow my fault that I'd been laid off. I kept wondering: if I'd been more active in the union, could I have done more to push a deal with the state? Or on the other hand, if I'd cozied up more to management, would they have let me stay on and dumped some other poor guy?

"And beyond feeling guilty, or maybe besides the guilt, I was just plain terrified. A few days ago, we'd been talking about how we could keep the kids in private school. Now that was like a joke; I was wondering how I could keep the house. And again, I felt guilty about that! What had we been thinking to take on such a big mortgage with our salaries? What had I been thinking? Had it just been arrogance? Or pride? Was I being paid back for so much good luck, for taking so much for granted? I half-believed that God was punishing me, and that made me feel more scared...I even questioned God for letting this happen to us."

Jeffrey smiles weakly, "I guess you could say my thoughts were not in a good place."

Perhaps not, but he was certainly in a place familiar to many people experiencing repeated misfortunes. Anger and fury are often accompanied and exacerbated by feelings of guilt, sorrow, grief, fear, and betrayal. Most people, including those who claim to have deep faith, find themselves wondering why God has allowed this to happen. Some report believing, almost against their will, that God has deliberately made this happen, and they wonder why.

One single mother who learned that both of her sons suffered from the same congenital illness, describes this feeling: "I kept thinking, 'OK, God, I guess you're mad at me or trying to tell me something. What did I do wrong? What can I do to make it up to you? What do I need to do for you to take this away?'

Trying to make deals with God in the midst of a crisis is also a common response. Jeffrey acknowledges going further than he likes to admit down that road. "I started talking to God, but it was not so much a prayer as a negotiation," he says, shaking his head sheepishly at the recollection. "I would say, 'OK, look, if it's me you're mad at, fine, but don't take it out on my wife and kids. Don't make them suffer. Give me some sickness or problem that won't affect them. I'll take it on gladly.' And I would have.

"Of course, that didn't work! But I still didn't get it. Instead, I changed my tune with God. Now, it was, 'Lord, if you really loved us, you wouldn't let this happen. Do you want me to yank my kids out of Catholic school? Do you want me to lose the house? Do you want Susan to cry herself to sleep at night? If you really love us, you'll get me my job back. If you really love us, show us!'

"You know, I'm ashamed when I think about it now, but I don't think it was a completely unique response. I'm only human, and when you believe in God, when you count on God, it's hard to avoid this kind of thinking when disaster strikes. Fortunately, God didn't hold my attitude against me."

Nor were any quick fixes provided. Faith, for most of us, is a long and sometimes challenging process. But as Susan and Jeffrey learned, it is a process that can lead to a purer, simpler, and more honest relationship with God.

Susan was the first to understand that she needed to use her anger as fuel for more positive action. Wasting her energy on the state, the union, or her fellow residents would not keep her family housed, fed, and safe. Although the union assured her they would eventually prevail and everyone who'd been laid off would get their jobs back with no reduction in wages or benefits, Susan was skeptical. She was not about to wait around. "One positive thing my rage did accomplish was to motivate me not to count on anything anybody said or promised!" she declares. "I'd already been-there, done-that...and it had not served us well!"

Recognizing Jeffrey's paralysis and bruised ego, Susan gave him lots of room while beginning to take steps of her own. She contacted a new bank about refinancing their mortgage or getting a second one to cover living costs. She insisted on answers from the state and her union representative on just how long she and Jeffrey would be eligible for unemployment compensation and benefits. Then she insisted that Jeffrey sit down with her to calculate how long they could survive before taking difficult steps like pulling the kids out of private school or putting the house up for sale.

"At first, it just made me feel worse, more inadequate, to see her doing all this," acknowledges Jeffrey. "But after awhile, I couldn't help but notice how she was turning her anger into actions to help us. It took me longer than it should have to get over my moping and feeling sorry for myself, but she definitely moved me in that direction. Also, the way she was looking at things in such a pragmatic, logical way helped me realize that this wasn't the complete disaster we'd originally believed. We did have some options. We did have some time. And we could make a viable plan for the future."

It was at the end of one night's long strategy session that Jeffrey hesitantly shared his feelings about God with his wife. He was concerned that Susan would think he'd lost his faith, or worse, that she'd lost hers and hadn't wanted to tell him. But Susan was not at all tentative in responding to her husband's "confession."

"I told him that what he was feeling was completely natural, and that God had not abandoned us, nor would he do so just because we were upset and confused right now," she says. She also suggested that they explore resources and classes at a nearby city church known for progressive programs and community activism. Jeffrey somewhat reluctantly agreed; Susan, though certain a faith community would give them a sense of stability, was not prepared for how much more they would receive.

It turned out that the urban parish had not locked itself in a stained glass tower while the rest of the world struggled with a failing economy, terrorism threats, and pervading uncertainty. The clerics and lay leaders had responded in "real time" to the challenges facing their parishioners and neighbors. In addition to programs on Bible study, church history, and spirituality, the church also offered a support group for the unemployed and underemployed, daycare for working families and those seeking work, a temporary shelter for the homeless, and an emergency food pantry. And these resources, notes Susan, were available to all who sought them.

"That's what really impressed me. We were not regular members of this church, but all we had to do was sign up and we were welcome," she says. "And they were doing a lot more than 'mouthing' platitudes. The employment support group, which Jeffrey immediately joined, offered resume writing workshops, job connections, interview techniques. You name it, if it was helpful from a practical point of view, they provided it. And to be honest, it was more than just the help; we felt a sense of belonging, of community there. After months of feeling like the frayed rope in a tug of war between the government and the union, between angry residents and rising taxes...well, it was nice just to be accepted as people in need."

Remember Joe and Rita from the previous chapter? Rita particularly empathizes with Susan's and Jeffrey's anger. "It is an exhausting emotion," says Rita, who often tries to bury her rage at what has happened to her brother, "but it can also seem like an unavoidable emotion, too. We're programmed to become angry when we're hurt and attacked or when those we love are hurt and attacked. It's almost like part of a survival instinct that kicks in."

Not everyone can follow Susan's example of transforming anger as a survival instinct into anger as energy to survive. Joe and Rita both acknowledge difficulty admitting and expressing their anger. Unlike Susan and Jeffrey, all their energy went into addressing Joe's pain and the myriad health and legal questions that followed his accident. Intense pain can make it hard to recognize any emotion besides the burning desire to have it go away. Joe frequently found himself too drained to begin to explore his own rage. It took therapy and serious self-examination for him to understand how much of his grief and depression were actually anger.

Even now he has a hard time talking about it. "I had the best imaginable life and I lost that life; had it taken from me, really. So I know I was angry. Am angry," he says, catching himself with a half-smile. "But I'd really rather not think about that. I'd rather work toward getting well and doing the things I've discovered I can do."

Rita, on the other hand, had a good idea of exactly how angry she was...and it scared her. "You know those therapists who advocate going out into the woods and screaming?" she asks with a chuckle. "Well, I was afraid if I tried it, I'd never stop screaming, and I'd never come back out of those woods!"

Yet sister and brother have both learned to reach out to others to help channel both their respective anger and pain. In addition to their parish and the support group, in which they both find themselves giving as much advice based on their own experience as accepting support from other members, they are moving in other directions. Rita has signed up for a yoga class, something she'd promised herself for months before actually doing it. She also plans on taking Italian lessons, and eventually, visiting the country her family came from. Joe is finding the courage to reach out to people besides those in his family, often driving others to the support group and staying in touch between meetings. During the warmer months, when his attacks are slightly less severe, he is trying to spend more time in simple social situations. His confidence is growing with each successful outing.

Jeffrey and Susan have also begun to see some opportunities in their situation. Long before their benefits ran out, Jeffrey had used a contact secured through the church's employment support group to get a job managing a retail store. Although the wages and benefits are not quite as good as his state job, he believes there are more opportunities for advancement. Because the store is part of a large chain, he and Susan realize that advancement may require a move in the future...or the decision not to move and keep the moderately paying job.

"At least we're more aware now, more ready to face what might come," says Susan, who works part-time from their home for a transcription service. She has heard rumblings that her department may be hiring back some of those laid off, but, as she puts it, "I'm not holding my breath! I think we've learned not to be so dependent on the rest of the world, and yet to be completely dependent on God.

"I mean, if we truly have faith, what choice do we really have?"

TALKING IT OVER WITH GOD

Father, I am so angry! I am angry that this has happened to me again. I am angry with everyone I believe is involved in this renewed crisis, and I'm even angry with those I know are not really involved! My family. My friends. My neighbors. My colleagues. My care-givers and doctors. Even strangers! None of them understand what I'm going through. In fact, I'm angry with anyone and everyone who seems happy, healthy, whole.

And Lord, I'm afraid to admit it, but sometimes I'm angry with you. Or at least confused about why you've allowed this to happen. There. I said it, and you haven't stricken me down the way I was raised to believe you might. And that itself is the reminder I need that old superstitions and old fears have no place in the new relationship you are offering me.

Help me to know that you are too great, too far beyond any paltry love or goodness I can imagine, to be offended by my puny anger. Help me to know that you love me regardless of my tragedy or my fury. Give me the courage of this conviction to use my confusion, sorrow, and anger to draw closer to you, to accept the new place you now offer me.

ASK YOURSELF

1. Has anger ever put you at a disadvantage when dealing with a renewed crisis?

2. Have you ever used anger to move yourself towards a positive resolution?

3. Do you agree with the suggestion that all anger is simply a form of fear?

Taking Further Action

• Rent the movie *Seabiscuit,* and note how the character of the jockey responds to the many losses in his life with wasteful rage before he learns to trust others and pursue realistic healing.

• Read the story of Esau and Jacob in the Book of Genesis, chapters 25—28 and 32—33, taking heart in how Esau eventually manages to put aside his rage and find resolution.

• Divide a blank page into two columns. On the top of one side, write, "Disadvantages of My Anger;" on the other side, write, "Advantages of My Anger." In the first column, list any ways in which your anger has kept you from dealing with your renewed crisis. Also list ways in which your anger may keep you from God. In the second column, list the ways you have—or could— use your anger as a fuel for positive action in dealing with your renewed crisis. Also, try to think of at least one way anger can help you turn, or return, to God. To move forward, focus on implementing the items in your second column.

CHAPTER FOUR

THE BLAME GAME

But now it has come to you, and you are impatient; it touches you, and you are dismayed. Think now, who that was innocent ever perished? Or where were the upright cut off? As I have seen, those who plow iniquity and sow trouble reap the same. Job 4:5, 7–8

Poor Job! Here he finds himself almost utterly destroyed; he has lost his children, his wealth, his own good health, even the respect and love of his wife. And his friends, instead of sympathizing and comforting him, are lining up to blame him for his ruined life. With friends like these...!

Unfortunately, the blame game is not unusual. Too often those facing a recurring tragedy find those around them all too willing to add the burden of blame to the crushing weight already oppressing them. Those who might be most expected to provide understanding and support are quickest to distance themselves with criticism or thinly veiled accusations ostensibly offered as "advice." Even more distressing, the fact that the crisis has returned seems to make these "advisors" even more convinced that they are justified in "blaming the victim."

We've all witnessed this type of condemning commentary, usually in a context far enough removed from personal tragedy that it's too easy to callously ignore such outrageous "blame statements." When a woman with what some judge to be a questionable reputation is raped, the violent crime may be dismissed because, "Well, who knows? She might have been asking for it. Have you seen how she dresses?" Or, "It's too bad, but really, what was she doing out that late anyway? The newspaper said she was leaving a bar. At that hour!?" Or, "I wouldn't let my daughter out of the house looking like that! I mean what did she expect would happen?"

Well, it's unlikely she expected to be raped, but that's hardly the point for such pontificators. And lest these judgments be dismissed as infrequent or the words of the uneducated and ignorant, there have been court cases where judges have meted out appallingly light sentences to convicted rapists, citing as justification the victim's habits, demeanor, or dress.

Such mean-spirited judgment is not reserved for the victims of crime. Entire political and governing philosophies are based on the insidious and sometimes unspoken belief that certain segments of the population deserve the poverty, squalor, and hunger that mar their lives. And while these opinions may remain unspoken in the era of political correctness, the stereotyping can still be heard—even if whispered. This group is characterized as "lazy." That group is dismissed as "welfare cheats." These people "breed like rabbits." Those people are "unnatural."

Equally as cruel are those who, like Job's critics, find reasons to blame those who have experienced repeated illness or personal crises. Yet all too often this is the first response of the so-called healthy to learning that a disease or syndrome has returned to burden an acquaintance. We hear it all the time: "It's too bad the cancer came back but she was advised to have a radical mastectomy the first time, and she refused because she didn't want to lose a breast. You can't just ignore the doctors like that." "Hey, I'm sorry the guy's liver is shot, but he should have stopped drinking years ago." "I know she says it's Chronic Fatigue Syndrome, but really, what is that anyway? I mean, everyone's tired, right?"

Such name-calling, presumptive blaming, and stereotyping is merciless. And quite often, it's simply wrong. But that doesn't seem to stop the self-righteous judges who make such assumptions. Why?

There are a number of reasons for this disturbing reaction. Some people are simply mean-spirited, uneducated, or bigoted. Often though, the motives are more complex. Perhaps the most pervading motive is distance; rather than acknowledge the fact that misfortune can befall anyone, some people would rather "blame" those who suffer, thus distancing themselves from the very prospect of that suffering. That way, they can reassure themselves that such a circumstance, illness, or tragedy could never happen to them. They can comfort themselves that they are immune if victims can be characterized as somehow bringing the trouble on themselves.

What they don't take into account is the impact of such "distancing" on the victim. Not only is that individual forced to shoulder the burden of a renewed crisis, they must also face the sting of blame and rejection from those around them. Cary experienced just this kind of searing abandonment when she was diagnosed with Lyme Disease. A little understood illness that can recur again and again, it can be hard to treat and brutally debilitating. With myriad symptoms that can cause everything from agonizing joint pain to exhaustion and a compromised immune system, its too frequent by-products include anxiety and depression.

Cary, a New York City scientist employed in research with a major drug company, grew severely ill with the disease. At first, her employer and colleagues were understanding, urging her to get the best possible treatment. But as the disease dragged on and no effective treatments were found, she was forced to give up her job. It wasn't long before her colleagues and some friends seemed to lose interest in her plight.

After working as a highly trained professional, supporting herself for all her adult life, she had to apply for disability income payments. With no help or encouragement to be found in the city she'd grown to love, she moved back to the small town where she'd been raised in upstate New York. "It was horrible," she recounts. "Not only was I in constant pain and unable to do simple things with symptoms that kept recurring no matter what the doctors said or did, I lost my work and my whole base of friends. I'd been accustomed to traveling all over the country, and suddenly some days I couldn't leave the house. The prevailing sense I got from people around me was, 'Why doesn't she just get over it? I mean, it's only a tick bite, right?'

"That attitude, as much as the disease itself, was just so painful. Even though I understood that people really didn't know what Lyme Disease was or what it could do, it still hurt me to be dismissed like that. It was like all that I'd achieved in my life to that point, all that I'd been as a person and a professional, was wiped out. As wiped out as I was feeling all the time!"

Cary even encountered this type of ambiguity among some of the doctors she approached for help. A pattern soon emerged: at first the practitioner or specialist would be very optimistic, recommending a specific course of treatment. But if the program didn't immediately work, the distancing started. "If I would call for a follow up, or if I was 'arrogant' enough to share any research I'd done on my own, based on my own knowledge about medicine and drugs, they would cool off really fast. It was as though I was trying to challenge them. And if their first treatment option wasn't completely successful, they acted like they'd done all they could and it was my fault. This made me all the more grateful for those doctors who have taken me seriously and offered different alternatives."

If it were not for those few doctors and therapists, Cary believes she might have completely lost hope. Certainly her decade-long experience has made her generally less trustful. "It's true what they say about finding out who your friends really are!" she says. "But that's not an easy lesson, especially not when you're trying to cope with the loss of everything you cared about: health, work, home, friends, travel—really, your whole life. The only real progress I've made is through God and prayer. These days, I pray about everything! I've often reached the point where I just completely give a situation to God."

For Cary, a well-educated and highly trained young scientist with a full, exciting life, it was devastating to suddenly feel like an outcast in her own world. Her world shrunk from one with few boundaries and obstacles to a small rental cottage on a lake in upstate New York. But the destructive impact of "distancing" and "blaming the victim" is not limited to successful people who are cut down by recurring trouble.

According to Father Joseph Wresinski, founder of the Fourth World Movement and subject of Gilles Anouil's book *The Poor Are the Church*, those living in abject poverty are also big losers in the blame game. In this book, what amounts to Anouil's extraordinary book-length interview with the priest, Fr. Wresinski observes that the very poor are acutely aware of how they are perceived and blamed for their circumstances, and that this knowledge contributes to the multiple sorrows and brutalities of their lives. To establish his intimate knowledge of how the destitute exist, Fr. Wresinski illustrates the impact of the added burden of societal opinion by describing his own impoverished childhood.

"My mother's passivity was similar to that of so many poor mothers whom I meet in destitute areas. Her anxiety about upsetting neighbors stemmed partly from fatigue but more so from fear. She was terrified of the police coming to arrest us…just like the mothers in emergency housing who are constantly afraid of people coming to do them harm. My mother would often complain to others about her torments, about me…about my bed-wetting. The whole neighborhood knew about it, which added to my shame. The poor do not hide their wounds. They have no strength left to mask the problems of an existence that exhausts them. For those of us who received charity, but never all that was due us, injustice was our daily fate."

Only much later after he'd committed his life to living with the very poor, Wresinksi notes, did he come to fully understand his mother and her fight against opinion and the culture of "charity" in poverty. "Only today do I understand the reserves of indignation and courage my mother needed to defend her children. She obstinately defended me again when the charity ladies of the parish conceived the idea of placing me in the orphanage. The plan was reasonable but very humiliating, both for children born in poverty and for their mothers, since poor children were raised separately from other children. My mother refused. She preferred to give up receiving any charity from this parish. Yet we were already excluded."

Wresinski posits that the mentality that distances society from the very poor contributes to the propagation of destitution. He suggests that abject poverty is not so much a self-fulfilling prophecy, as many people would like to believe in order to remove themselves from vulnerability to that state—as well as the responsibility to address it—but a kind of "other-fulfilling" prophecy. In other words, because impoverished people know what others think of them, they feel even more ashamed, isolated, and doomed to experience the same recurring crises.

So how much does the blame game truly add to the already crushing weight of those in trouble? It may be impossible to gauge. At first glance it appears that individuals like Cary must shoulder a different burden from that forced on entire communities of people who are plagued by stereotyping critics. After all, Cary was a highly successful member of society, who only felt the sting of rejection after illness forced her to "drop out" of the life she'd known. On the other hand poor people and racial minorities are, as Fr. Wresinski points out, outcasts from their birth. It is perhaps a matter of deciding which is worse: to have lost everything, including society's good opinion; or to have never had anything including that good opinion.

In the final analysis, it may not matter which is more painful since both these groups confront the same debilitating sense of being blamed, isolated, and "turned away" by others. They share the knowledge that such ostracization adds immeasurably to the already painful tragedies they wrestle with every day. As Cary points out, it weakens the will and often results in plummeting self-confidence. "I get to the point where I get so sick and tired of feeling sick and tired," she says wearily, "but I really don't know who to turn to. Some days I just can't bring myself to feel very trusting or hopeful."

How can people already struggling with a recurring crisis recover from this sense of alienation and abandonment?

Sometimes honestly confronting those who "blame the victim" is a way to recover some sense of dignity. Job does this, more out of frustration and anger than as a way to seek resolution. His outrage is palpable as he turns in hurt astonishment to his so-called friends and questions how they could attack him when he's already so decimated. They have no answer, except to defend themselves in the name of righteousness; it is only when God intervenes that the critics are cowed.

When Susan, much like Job, spoke up when an acquaintance was maligning state workers, she discovered that such an assertive response might even result in the fault-finder coming to understand his or her cruelty. Susan simply told the woman how deeply her words had cut and how unfair they were to the majority of hard-working government employees. Susan recalls the encounter: "She was stunned. At first I thought she would defend herself, but there must have been the right combination of anger and near-tears in my attitude, because she stopped speaking and just looked at me. She actually blushed! Then she muttered an apology and walked quickly away. But I had the feeling I'd gotten through to her. And, most important, I felt better!"

Cary's experience has been somewhat different on the occasions when she's stood up to a doctor or professional who has faulted her for wanting to participate in her own healing. "Mostly the response has been one of 'How dare you question me? What do you know about it?'" she says. And while she may wish to aggressively confront this disturbing attitude, she finds herself in the uncomfortable position of still being dependent on the medical profession. Unlike Susan, or even Job, Cary can't easily walk away from those who doubt or question her. Maintaining her dignity and self-esteem can become a battle as wrenching as the one to regain her health.

In *The Poor Are the Church*, Fr. Wresinski again returns to the example of his mother to show how violently maligned classes of people must struggle for their rights and dignity. He writes, "I began to support my family before the age of five. Every morning for almost eleven years, my mother called me for the seven o'clock Mass. It took me at least ten minutes to run to the chapel…in the winter I was cold and frightened of the dark. Whether it was windy or rainy, I walked…almost bent over double, half asleep, sometimes shouting with rage. I don't think I ever missed a single one of those morning duties. Mother must have been greatly in need when it came to feeding us, to accept sending such a young boy out onto the streets every day. I must also have been aware of her feeling of helplessness, when I took on this duty without bitterness or anger against God."

Fr. Wresinski realized early on that although society might categorize and isolate him and his family, God did not. He understood what Job discovered and what all of us who are targets in the blame game must learn: God does not blame, ostracize, mock, or separate from us. Indeed, as we read in Job, God is harsh with those who do practice such dispassionate cruelty.

There are times in our lives, when pain and loneliness return, threatening to overwhelm us. Then, now, God is our one and only comfort. And as it turns out, happily, this is the only comfort we truly need.

TALKING IT OVER WITH GOD

Lord, I am so hurt. I'm hurt by this burden that has been laid again across my back. I'm hurt by the weight and the feel and the exhausting drain of it. But I'm hurt, maybe even as much, by the attitude of some people around me. I see their faces, that look in their eyes, their whispers, how they avoid me in the store or even in church. They act like I'm contagious.

They seem to think that this is my fault; that I brought this trouble back into my life; that I somehow messed up and now this has befallen me as a kind of punishment. Some of them even think it's OK to tell me this outright…like they're doing me a favor by pointing out my faults. And some of them are people who claim to love me! God help me, because sometimes I can't help but feel this way myself! I am filled with wearying doubt. My self-esteem has evaporated. All this blaming makes me wonder if I am at fault!

Lord, I know this is dangerous, weakened thinking. I know it is the kind of thinking that erodes faith. I know you are not punishing me. I know all this, but some days I don't feel it. Sustain and comfort me in these hurtful, vulnerable times, my Lord! I sometimes feel that you are all I have. Now I know that you are all I need.

ASK YOURSELF

1. Have you ever tried to distance yourself from someone experiencing tragedy by somehow blaming that person, even if you did it silently?
2. Has anyone ever blamed you when you were struggling with a painful burden?
3. Have you ever used self-blame to cut yourself off from God?

Taking Further Action

• Read Gilles Anouil's *The Poor Are the Church*, featuring Father Joseph Wresinski. Be aware of when, how, and why Fr. Wresinski's observations make you uncomfortable.

• Read the Book of Job, focusing on the cruel self-righteousness of Job's companions and, especially, God's response to those so-called friends.

• Consider whether you have ever blamed someone for their troubled circumstances. Honestly examine your motives. Did you do it to keep a safe distance between yourself and the hurting person? Were you trying to reassure yourself that the same thing could never happen to you? Were you trying to avoid the hard work of helping another?

Whatever your motives, you can take a healing action now. If you criticized the individual face-to-face, especially if you did it under the guise of offering "advice," apologize to the person now. Confess your motive, and ask for forgiveness. If you criticized the person to others or just to yourself, contact the individual now and offer words of encouragement and support. Offer to help in any way you can...without telling the person precisely what sort of help you think they need!

CHAPTER FIVE

THE COMPULSION TO REPEAT

The Lord said to Moses, "Your brother Aaron shall tell Pharaoh to let the Israelites go out of his land...and I will multiply my signs and wonders in the land of Egypt. When Pharaoh does not listen to you, I will lay my hand upon Egypt and bring my people the Israelites...out of the land of Egypt by great acts of judgment.

Exodus 7:2–4

Not only was Pharaoh obstinate, he was repeatedly obstinate. And his insistence on repeating a mistake that had already brought his people great suffering resulted in repeated doom and disaster for himself and his nation. As we saw in the previous chapter, playing the blame game in the face of renewed tragedy can be extremely debilitating. Playing the avoidance game, on the other hand, can impede and even prevent progress and healing.

Just as Pharaoh played the avoidance game by refusing to examine his own complicity in the recurring disasters of his world, so do some people today who experience repeated difficulties. Sadly, the results can be just as devastating.

41

A hard-driving, "type-A" businessman who eats unhealthy food, doesn't make time to exercise, and keeps himself under great stress has a heart attack. The attack stops him dead in his tracks; actually, it nearly stops him dead, period. For the first time in his life, he actually listens to someone besides himself. He pays as much attention to his doctors as he has paid in the past to his company's profit and loss statements. He listens attentively to all their advice, remembering the excruciating and very recent pain of having a stint put in his chest. He nods aggressively: yes, he will cut the fat in his diet and eat fresh vegetables, he will exercise daily, he will spend more time at home relaxing, he will get his priorities in order, and he does understand that sixteen-hour days can no longer be one of them.

Then he goes home. The memory of the pain fades a bit. He gets a little bored on his daily walks and bicycle rides. The book he's reading—the first novel in over a decade—isn't as interesting as the *New York Times Book Review* suggested it would be. The new food his wife is preparing has too much crunch and not enough flavor. His worried wife and family are irritating him with so much hovering.

Finally, he can go back to work. Right, right, he knows: only part-time. Sure. But part-time compared with his previous schedule could be up to fifty hours a week, right? OK, OK, he's just kidding, but at least he can do an easy forty hours a week, right? Of course he can. After a week, he finds himself forced to reprimand his assistant for trying to keep him on an easy schedule. His assistant, after all, is supposed to do his bidding, not his wife's. The assistant, appropriately chastised and wishing to keep his job, makes no further attempt to reduce his boss's work load or keep his schedule. So he misses an appointment with his cardiologist and a few therapy sessions. Well, he'll get to them next week.

A week later, his company's quarterly earnings report comes out. This is disgraceful! Look what happens when he's out of commission for a few measly weeks! Never mind that the economy is weak, his company will not perform this poorly! It never has in the past;

it certainly will not in the future. He'll need to schedule several dinner meetings with his top staff members and their clients. Make the reservations at the high end steak house around the corner, he tells his silent assistant, might as well eat well while we hash this out. And make sure they bring around those contraband Cuban cigars with the brandy and dessert. People will need cheering up.

Three months later he's back in the intensive care unit. He collapses after a heavy meal celebrating his company's comeback quarter. Earnings were up 17 percent. His heart is now permanently damaged. He's in danger of having one or even a series of strokes. The stint is not working anymore. Chances of a complete recovery are slim.

But if he should recover, what will he do next? Certainly he will truly change his ways this time; no sensible human being could ignore such a second warning. Right?

Too often we become addicted to old patterns of behavior, no matter how damaging those patterns may be. This can be true for attitudes and interactions as well as for health habits. Dr. Alice Miller, an internationally known psychoanalyst and author, frequently discusses how the "compulsion to repeat" can result in people finding themselves again and again in the same negative circumstances. Miller uses the phrase to refer to how people can spend their lives making the same bad decisions, probably because they've never responded honestly to something that happened in their original family. But regardless of the reason for the "compulsion to repeat," it can wreak havoc in our lives and relationships.

In her book, *The Drama of the Gifted Child*, Miller describes the case of a woman, who because she was not able to get the kind of love and acceptance she needed as a child, was determined to find a partner who would provide for her needs. Except that, instead of exploring her sense of loss, she continually sought out men who were not capable of offering the love and understanding she yearned for. Miller writes that the patient, perpetuating this debilitating pattern, began dating a man "to whom she wrote long letters trying to explain the path she had taken in her therapy…she succeeded in overlooking all signals of his incomprehension and increased her efforts even more, until at last she was forced to recognize that she had again found a father substitute and that this was the reason she had been unable to give up her hopes of at last being understood. This…brought her agonizingly sharp feelings of shame."

And shame, of course, simply causes more pain and self-abuse, making the recurring behaviors and resulting crises harder to clarify and eliminate. The trick here is to not fall victim to the blame/shame games while remaining clear-headed and honest enough to examine our true desires and actual behaviors. Without this kind of gentle but honest exploration, the compulsion to repeat can cause all kinds of havoc and instigate every possible sort of second strike.

A second divorce may be the result of not changing behaviors or attractions that destroyed the first marriage. Refusing to improve poor health and lifestyle habits may bring on a second heart attack or other health crisis. Bringing an unreasonable, uncooperative attitude to a new job after being laid off for those very reasons will ensure the loss of the second job. Skipping AA or Alanon meetings may signal a return to addictions. The list, unfortunately, can go on and on.

Miller suggests that the compulsion to repeat can be broken by an honest assessment of our emotions and motives. "Seen in this way the compulsion to repeat is a great opportunity. It can be resolved when the feelings in the present situation can be felt and clarified. If use is not made of this opportunity, if its message is ignored, the compulsion to repeat will continue without abating for the person's entire lifetime, although its form may change. What is unconscious cannot be abolished by proclamation or prohibition. One can, however, develop sensitivity toward recognizing it and begin to experience it consciously, and thus eventually gain control over it."

Perhaps one of the most damaging behavioral repetitions is when we automatically react to a second strike in the same negative way we responded to the first. While it's natural to fall back on old ways in the face of a stunning, upsetting event, it's not always helpful. If those old ways impede recovery and healing, this particular compulsion to repeat can be downright dangerous.

Unfortunately the old ways are familiar and easy to draw upon. Raised with certain beliefs and coping mechanisms, we almost habitually return to those learned behaviors, right or wrong, in times of crisis. For example, some of us were left with the impression that God punishes us by causing bad things to happen when we've done something wrong. Even if we've grown to know that's not true, we may be programmed to "boomerang" back to such wrong-headed and hurtful thinking. Thus, our swift and automatic response to a second strike might very well be (as it probably was with the first strike): God is angry with me. Or, God has abandoned me. Or, God doesn't love me. Or even, God is trying to teach me a lesson.

This compulsion to repeat faith-eroding thoughts can also lead us to feel betrayed by God, particularly if we've convinced ourselves that God "solved" this problem for us the last time. "How then," we cry in confusion, "could God have 'sent' this back into our lives?" Well, the truth—and we know it even if we don't always feel it—is that God certainly didn't bring this thing into our life, not the first time, not this time, and not the time when it may return. Still, our habits, beliefs, and superstitions often run deep, all but compelling us to respond to a recurring trouble with anger, guilt, or a sense that God has betrayed us.

If these negative responses come shooting to the surface, don't despair. At the same time, don't give in to them. They didn't help last time, they certainly won't help this time. You can break this compulsion to repeat. Remember Miller's suggestion that addressing real feelings and fears "in the moment" can reduce the compulsion to repeat unhelpful or damaging behaviors. Further, she explains that the more conscious a person is of a compulsion to repeat, the more able he or she will be to recognize it and eliminate it.

In other words if you know that your "programmed" response to shock, pain, and fear is to think God is angry and punishing you, then you must try to identify this tendency; remind yourself that it is wrong and damaging; and remember that God is waiting to love and comfort you. Don't forget to give yourself a break by acknowledging that it is natural to feel terrified and hurt at this moment.

Or if you know that your automatic response to a recurring problem is frustration, anger, and a sense that God—and maybe everyone else—has betrayed you, then you should work to recognize your instant reaction as false and damaging. Remember that God is with you and has already forgiven you and banish your guilt by realizing that it is normal to make fear and uncertainty into anger and confusion.

We are all are shaped by circumstances: genetics, upbringing, religious traditions, political beliefs, education, financial state, race, and ethnicity, not to mention who we love and who loves us. Thus, all of us inherit or develop compulsions to repeat. These can be necessary to survival and growth; just as often they can be obstacles. The harmful compulsions are those most likely to impede our journey to God, faith, good health, peace of mind, and strong loving relationships. Recognizing and controlling these compulsions are vital steps in confronting recurrent crises and developing an honest, trusting bond with God.

TALKING IT OVER WITH GOD

Lord, although I should not listen to anyone who would blame me for my circumstances, I understand that I must look into myself to determine whether I am repeating behaviors that keep me from healing, or worse, that keep me from you. Help me to honestly assess my life and choices. Help me to do this without debilitating self-recrimination or crippling self-pity.

Be with me, Lord, as I undertake this honest examination. Let me realize that, as much as I may dread this exploration of my actions and motives, it is a way to give myself more completely to you. Because when I'm finished, it is you to whom I must turn to learn new and healthier ways.

Only you can draw me away from my own negative patterns and thoughts. Only you can bring me the insight to change. Only you can lead me to the people and resources who will help me to change. Lord, let me have the courage to begin, and then to follow.

ASK YOURSELF

1. Have you ever contributed to your own recurring problems by repeating negative behaviors?

2. In your faith journey, do you find yourself making promises and resolutions that are nearly impossible to keep, thus setting yourself up for feelings of failure?

3. Can you identify ways in which the "compulsion to repeat" untenable behaviors have resulted in regional discord or war?

TAKING FURTHER ACTION

• Read Alice Miller's *Drama of the Gifted Child*, noting particularly her definition/description of the compulsion to repeat.

• Read Exodus chapters 7—14, which feature Pharaoh's unyielding and ultimately devastating compulsion to repeat.

• Use the "compulsion to repeat" in a positive way. You've probably already identified repeated behaviors which bring you repeated troubles. Now make a list of behaviors that promote success and healing in your life. In many cases they will simply be the opposite of those negative behavior. These positive actions might include exercising regularly, praying daily, reading inspirational material for fifteen minutes every day, scheduling regular appointments with a therapists and keeping those appointments, visiting a local convalescent home, spending time with your spouse or children, sleeping at least seven hours a night, avoiding gossips and mean-spirited people, seeking out positive and spiritual people, and/or spending more time listening than talking in a conversation. After you finish your list, pick one and do it. Again. And again. When you've successfully established a "compulsion to repeat" with this one item, go on to the next. And repeat.

Chapter Six

PRAYER WARRIORS

She prayed to the Lord God of Israel, and said: "O my Lord, you only are our king; help me, who am alone and have no helper but you, for my danger is in my hand."   Esther 14:3–4

For a traditional Hebrew girl, Esther's life to this point had been one long series of devastating events. She was orphaned, left to an uncle to be raised; her people had been conquered; she was given or sold into sexual slavery; and finally she was forced to marry the man who had subjugated her nation. Now, at this desperate juncture when she's discovered that her husband, the ruthless foreign conqueror, is about to annihilate her entire nation, she beseeches the Lord with simple, stirring faith.

Frequently people who experience repeated tragedies reach this point of overwhelming loneliness, of near despair. We can even reach a point where we are beyond Esther's solitary prayer; a point where we haven't the heart or the faith to turn so completely to God and utter such wrenching, trusting words. While Esther prays with complete humility and dependence upon God, we may be so leveled by a current crisis that we can't even summon the courage to become a humble supplicant. A second strike can precipitate a very real prayer crisis; we may fall into negative thinking, telling ourselves that if our prayers had been working, God would not have let this happen again. And since it did happen, we cry out, how can prayer possibly be effective? Both the words and the hope slip away.

What then?

Prayer is powerful; the hope and practice of it should never be abandoned. But what happens when we just don't know what to say, what to do? Or when we simply don't think we can fashion the words to match our needs? When our tongues are tied by fear and disappointment? When we can't imagine that the Lord will bother to listen to us? When we worry that God's already stopped hearing us at all?

That's when we turn to the prayer warriors. These are the people in our histories and our lives who pray mightily and as easily as they breathe. Prayer warriors usually fall into two categories: people who have spoken through the pages of history, tradition, and religion; and people in our own lives. Regardless of whether prayer warriors are legendary or living, they can help dispel prayer dry spells through their examples and their active prayer.

Legendary prayer warriors, like Esther, may be the easiest to emulate; it is merely a matter of imitation. At first this may feel uncomfortable, even vaguely ridiculous: the idea of memorizing and mimicking another's prayer. What's the point, after all, of just hijacking someone else's words? Yet how is that different from the way every child first learns to pray? Learning or memorizing prayer is the first stepping stone to communicating with God.

When we are too young and inexperienced to know how to speak directly to God, we "say our prayers," those holy and righteous words we are first taught, usually as children. If we learned to rely on those prayers before our relationship with God matured into a more personal bond, why not use memorized prayers now if we find ourselves unable to resume our normal conversation with God?

So those prayers of childhood, many of which are still said at

Mass or during various religious services, can be valuable resources now. We can certainly return to them and take comfort in the cadence and recitation of the words. Millions, perhaps billions, of people over the ages have been consoled and even healed simply by intoning the repetitive prayers of the rosary.

Let's not forget that Jesus was one of the first prayer warriors, providing us the words of the Lord's Prayer after the disciples ask him how to pray. Imagine saying the Lord's Prayer, slowly, focusing on each phrase and what it can mean in this time of trouble. Didn't Jesus say that this one prayer is all we really need? A person in pain may simply start with one or two lines, saying them aloud, and then meditating on what each line, or even word, means.

We can also model our words on those of other legendary prayer warriors we've come to know through books and tradition. The Bible is one of the best resources, whether we are seeking prayers to recite, or simply a philosophy of prayer that can be expressed in no more than a line or two. Esther's prayer is a tremendous example of this: "O My Lord...help me who am alone and have no helper but you, for my danger is in my hand." For someone who's been rendered silent by a recurring tragedy, this just about says it all, expressing loneliness, despair, complete dependence on God, and the feeling—right or wrong—that this crisis is a crushing weight that must be borne alone.

Another wondrously evocative model of the philosophy of prayer is the parable of the Pharisee and the tax collector in the gospel of Luke, offered by Jesus as an example of the kind of prayer that God will hear and accept. The tax collector, whom Jesus compares favorably to those who pray with a great show of public piety, merely beats his breast and begs God to have mercy on him, a sinner. Readers can only imagine his grief and repentance; he apparently feels that he is the least worthy of all God's creatures, and yet Jesus declares that God hears him before others who are less despairing. Indeed, Jesus has little praise for the Pharisee, who prays with great confidence, almost boasting about his wonderful, fortune-filled life. The humble, sorrowful tax collector is clearly on the right path. Prayer cannot be simpler than this, and many people who experience deep troubles can identify with this man.

For those who feel comfortable reading prayers, the psalms, mostly written by King David, provide myriad possibilities for returning to prayer. No matter what difficulty we might be facing, it's a fair bet that David faced it in some form and wrote about it. In David we have a fallible, vulnerable man who has been made into a king and given more responsibilities and challenges than any political or religious leader since Moses. David feels his burdens as a king and his failures as a man so keenly that we cannot help but identify with him. As a result, he left us with a wealth of psalms that can be studied, read, and recited as prayers in our own times of distress.

Some of history's most powerful prayer warriors are not necessarily part of a familiar religious tradition. For those who feel their customary prayers and models have failed them, these prayer warriors can literally be a Godsend. Those saints and holy men and women referred to as "mystics" offer unusual examples of prayer and lifestyles fashioned around their devotion to God. Books describing the lives of saints often emphasize the contributions of the mystics, and many are subjects of inspiring biographies.

Generations have turned to Mahatma Gandhi as a model of peace and determined faith during brutal times. The life and work of Martin Luther King, Jr. were modeled on Gandhi's teachings. Millions of people have proven that one need not be a Hindu to greatly benefit from the active prayer that is yoga, the Hindu path to God. The Buddha's teachings have comforted many who have suddenly found this world impossible to navigate. These and numerous other examples can be found in Huston Smith's acclaimed book, *The World's Religions*.

The prayer warriors of our personal lives are as valuable, though in some cases more challenging, as those found in history and tradition. These individuals are more challenging because they are actually "in our face" about prayer. They are the ones who won't let us forget our need for God and our need to communicate with God. They are the ones who will do it for us when we simply don't have the heart. In that way, they are both instigators to prayer and examples of it. By holding up our end of things, they also transform themselves into living bridges back to the Lord.

Prayer warriors can be quiet, stable influences, or they can be indefatigable faith-criers, continually and loudly proclaiming God's love. They relentlessly remind us that God has not abandoned us even if we feel abandoned, and that God has not stopped loving us even if we feel unloved. I've been blessed to have both kinds of prayer warriors, and one of my most constant advocates combines the best of both styles. She also leads by example; the numerous crises she'd lived through provided her with immediate legitimacy in my dry, aching eyes.

Sylvia came into my life well before my second strike. She wrote to me shortly after I'd published a series in *Daily Guideposts* detailing my first experience with melanoma. Her daughter was in the process of becoming a cancer survivor at that time, and Sylvia had read my series. She wanted me to pray for her daughter and her family. Of course, I responded, in the flush of good health and after a number of clean biopsies. I could afford to be magnanimous. God had brought me through my crisis, I believed, so that I could help others through their pain. The idea that God had sent Sylvia to me, and not necessarily the reverse, never entered my over-confident mind.

Sylvia's daughter continued to heal. After exchanging a number of letters, Sylvia and I began talking on the phone occasionally. She lived in North Carolina, I lived in Connecticut, but our conversations might have been those of next door neighbors. Eventually, Sylvia ventured a suggestion: did I want to have a more formal prayer fellowship? Intrigued, I asked her what she meant. She said we would schedule an evening, once every two weeks, to talk much like we'd been talking, and also to pray. This didn't seem like any monumental change to me, and I readily agreed.

It was more than monumental. It was spirit-saving.

By the time I learned about my new cancer, Sylvia and I had been having fellowship steadily for over a year. From our very first "meeting," as she called it, I'd been absolutely astonished and delighted by her style of prayer. It was like nothing I, a rather unadventurous Catholic, had ever experienced. Her prayer was so full of joy, so full of abiding, unalterable faith. There was nothing bland or complacent about it. Instead, she simply spoke to God, but in a way that was so full of life and love and trust that it virtually mesmerized me. I would close my eyes as she would begin, losing myself in her voice, putting myself in her shoes, believing that God was right there in the room.

She would tell God how good he was, that she knew he would never, ever let us down. The first part of her prayer was nothing but thanking God: for our fellowship, for her family, for my family, for traveling blessings, for healing, for peaceful times in her country, Sierra Leone. You name it, she'd find a way to thank God for it. She prayed for terrorists and murderers in the same breath that she prayed for their victims. She prayed for peace and justice and protection, all at once. She seemed to have no doubt that all this was possible with God. She did not negotiate or complain; she seldom asked for specific outcomes. The trust evident in her words was all-encompassing.

Our fellowship calls always started with a lengthy exchange of news, and we grew to be good friends this way. But when it came to prayer time, I was almost embarrassed to offer mine during those first few calls after I'd heard Sylvia pray! My words seemed so paltry, so halting, compared to hers. Eventually, I caught some of her spirit (who could not??), and my prayer became more hopeful and expansive, more expressive of the love I'd always felt for God. But always, I asked to go first, because I wanted her prayers to be the last words echoing in my mind when we hung up. She has this extraordinary, lilting voice that sings of her native Sierra Leone, and often her prayer became my soothing lullaby.

Some of Sylvia's phrases, graced with the absolute beauty of her language and cadence, stayed with me and thrilled me every day. "Lord, we know you are a good God." "Father, we believe that you will bring this to a resolution because you are not a God of unfinished business." "Let us do all that we do unto your glory, Father." "Lord, you know that Marci's husband is traveling tonight. Do thou protect him. Do thou bring him home safely. We leave him into your kind care, Father."

This was my favorite: we leave him (or her, or them, or this) into your kind care, Father. Long before I knew how much I would come to need this one line of prayer, it greatly comforted me. It bespoke a kind of trust that I'd always thought unattainable. It did not demand a certain result. It left no room for hedging, negotiating, back-sliding. It simply left everything to God, in a way that most people cannot imagine. And she meant it! Though she'd lived a life that was as full of sorrow and loss as it had been of joy, she absolutely believed that all was in God's hands, all to the good! That's what I came to understand over the course of our friendship, and in that, too, I took great solace.

When I called her after the biopsy had turned up a new cancer, I could barely speak. I did, however, immediately begin telling her how "good" the situation was: earliest stage, surgically removed, doctor confident. It was as though by telling her I could convince myself all over again. The truth is I was badly shaken by this second strike. I found myself wondering what I'd done wrong, whether I'd offended God somehow. I'd felt so close to God, especially after the first bout with cancer: had I just been kidding myself? Was I really worthy of true healing? My heart and mind were telling me one thing, that God loved me and wanted to comfort me, but my gut was moaning that old despairing dirge about sin and punishment.

And so I recited to Sylvia all the doctor's positive words.

Sylvia listened quietly to my dull-voiced litany of good news, but good news was never a surprise for her. She believed that everything, one way or another, was good news. She also believed, unwaveringly, that I would be healed. And while my doctor would certainly be a tool, God was the healer. She started right away with a new series of prayer phrases; in fact at this point, her very speech became a constant prayer. Everything she said to me was meant to bring me close to God, to keep the divine, healing presence clear in my mind and body.

For the next three months, as I underwent biopsy after biopsy, a new group of Sylvia's tremendously powerful prayer lines whispered in my ears. "Lord, we know you are healing Marci, that those spots will disappear!" "Father, we know the doctor will find nothing in this new biopsy." "Good God, we lift Marci up to you in prayer." And my favorite of Sylvia's refrains was not a formal prayer at all. She would simply say, a dozen times a day when necessary, "It will be all right."

Now this wasn't said in a dismissive way, as in "I need to hang up now." And it was not said in a furtive way, as in "I have no idea what to say so I'm falling back on this." Nor was it said in a sweetly optimistic way, as in "Oh, live in the moment and notice the beautiful spring flowers and the little bees and butterflies in our perfect world." No. When Sylvia said, "It will be all right," she said it in a matter-of-fact voice as though any other outcome was inconceivable. And she meant it.

Even better, I came to feel she might be right.

When the numbness receded enough for me to really understand what she meant, at first, it terrified me. She meant that with God, everything would always be right, that no matter the outcome, all would be well. Her words were an acknowledgment that we had no control—actually, that I had no control. My only peace would come when I accepted that and came to believe that God's plan was in place. Next to that, all my plans amounted to nothing. This initially paralyzed me with fear; after all, she was talking about the kind of ultimate faith that I had only ascribed to certain saints. I could hardly wrap my bruised mind around this concept: that this sort of faith was possible for deeply flawed mortals. Like me. And then, I felt a glimmer of something hiding just beyond that massive ocean of fear.

Relief.

The idea that God loved me so much that I could stop worrying about the actual state and condition of my life was breath-taking. At the same time it frightened me to even think the words: That God loved me beyond health and illness, beyond achievement and failure, beyond friends and family—beyond life and death. Though I felt the prospect of relief cascading through me, I knew I wasn't yet able to bathe under such a searingly pure waterfall.

Relief and terror played hide and seek in my mind for quite some time. They still do most days. Sylvia had shown me that it was possible to believe so deeply in God that the only result of such faith would be to release the need for control, for specific outcomes. Not only had she shown me, she believed it herself. And with all I'd come to learn about her life, I knew she was a living testimony to this belief. She'd experienced just about every kind of recurring crisis imaginable. She'd lost her husband and son. She'd been in Sierra Leone when her country fell victim to a devastating war. She'd seen her home shot up, and she'd begged insurgents not to burn it. She'd seen her brother kidnapped, her friends and beloved staff members killed, her nation rent with rage and violence. She'd journeyed through cancer with her daughter.

This was the woman who was my prayer warrior, the woman who insisted, "It will be all right."

I had to, at least, listen.

TALKING IT OVER WITH GOD

Lord, sometimes I feel unable to pray. Of course you know that better than anyone, and though I know you don't judge the quality or quantity of my prayer, I feel badly about my prayer paralysis. I wish I could pray. I wish I knew what to say. I wish I could do more than merely recite the prayers I learned as a child. But sometimes, in the face of my anguish as I face this new old crisis, I just don't know what to say. Lord, help me to know that silence, offered to you, is a form of prayer.

Teach me that your blessed silence in return is no rejection, but truly a soft embrace of love and acceptance. Help me to remember Esther's simple and stirring request. Let me recall the humble sinner crouching in the back of the temple and eloquently begging for your mercy. Allow me, Lord, to relax into silent prayer or to softly repeat these honest supplications. Teach me the value of turning to prayer partners and prayer warriors; those good people who will pray with me and for me. Restore, O Lord, my faith in prayer: mine, theirs, and ours.

ASK YOURSELF

1. When you are in need, do you turn to God as a first resort, or as a last resort?
2. Have you ever been in a situation where you asked someone of deep faith to pray for or with you?
3. Are you satisfied with your own prayer life?

TAKING FURTHER ACTION

• Sing or read a copy of the quintessential Christmas song, *O Holy Night*, noting particularly the deep dependence on the Lord and universal yearning for the divine presence that is inherent in every line.

• Read the Book of Esther, attending to the many serious setbacks Esther faces in her life and how she responds with utter faith in God and God alone.

• Consider a difficult situation in your life right now. Imagine that every person and resource you would normally turn to for help is out of reach. You cannot immediately turn to a doctor, a spouse, a priest, a police officer, a lawyer, the internet. Don't panic about this! Now allow yourself to know that God and God alone is available to help you.

With that in mind, pray the simple prayer of Esther that heads this chapter. Repeat it again and again if necessary. Allow the calm of depending on God to flow over and through you. Remain peaceful for as long as you wish, and in that state of mind, also pray for God to guide and enlighten all those to whom you will, indeed, turn to for help in this matter. Acknowledge that God is in charge of everything.

CHAPTER SEVEN

TOO MUCH TO LOSE

Isaac said to his father Abraham..."The fire and the wood are here, but where is the lamb for a burnt offering?" Abraham said, "God himself will provide the lamb for a burnt offering, my son."

Genesis 22:7–8

How could Abraham have answered so calmly, and from our perspective at least, so deceptively? He knew that God had instructed him to sacrifice Isaac, so how could he have lied so cruelly to his son? Could it be that Abraham wasn't lying; that even then, when he had so much to lose, Abraham trusted God to restore all?

That Abraham. Talk about an exemplary prayer warrior!

For those embittered by multiple losses, it is easy to think that only a patriarch of God could have such faith. After all, Abraham had actually hung out with God! They were practically old buddies, so maybe it was easier for him to believe in such benefice. But who could expect that kind of faith from mere humans who aren't so well acquainted with the Almighty? It's just too much to ask, right?

Granted, that's an understandable attitude, but it's also a way of rejecting the fact that God does indeed ask such faith of those facing losses. Furthermore, theology and history are both replete with records of ordinary people who do respond to unspeakable tragedy with unfathomable faith.

Jesus's mother, Mary, is probably the best known example of someone who never doubts God despite searing losses. From the beginning, when God tells this mere child she will bear a divine infant, to the end, when she—accompanied only by other women who are themselves well-acquainted with loss—watches and waits at the foot of her son's cross, she is the model of unwavering faith. Whatever sorrows—and they were many and excruciating—she accepted, Mary is never seen to falter.

Her losses were extraordinary. When no more than a girl, she lost her standing and place in her community because she agreed to become pregnant with the Christ. The outrage of the Hebrew villagers at a young girl, already betrothed in marriage, turning up pregnant was nothing like the response communities may have today to a pregnant thirteen year old. Back then, in that strict religious environment, there would be no blaming the man who got her pregnant; no blaming her parents; no blaming the state and local child protection agencies. There would be no understanding for the girl, how she was raised, whether she'd been abused, what she lacked in material goods or social standing. There would have been nothing but sheer condemnation, perhaps even stoning, and at the very least an ignoble divorce that would forever ostracize her from her people.

Even when Joseph, given direction in a divine dream, agreed to take Mary as his wife, she had already been sent away by her family to prevent the villagers from avidly watching her growing belly. Who, besides Joseph, who himself had to be convinced by God, would have believed her claim that she was still a virgin, that she was pregnant by the Spirit of the Most High?

What Mary didn't lose in terms of community and place by showing up pregnant, she lost immediately thereafter when her new husband was compelled to take her away to Bethlehem for a census. With everything that had happened to that point, there's no doubt that Mary knew she was leaving her village forever. When Joseph lifted her thin girl's body, swollen with the Christ child, onto the foal that would carry her to the stable so far away, she knew she was not coming back. What did she feel when she gazed into the mournful face of her mother, who must have still been perplexed and hurt by her daughter's condition? What did she feel when she bade farewell to the father who could not protect her from her fate? Did he even respond to her cries and waves?

Before she was even well into her teens, then, Mary had lost her reputation, her community, her home, and her family. The losses had only just begun. Driven immediately after Jesus's birth into another nation altogether by the cruelty of her son's enemies, she lost any hope of safety and stability. Imagine her thoughts as she realized that the agonizing separation from all she'd known, and the isolated, frightening, painful birth was just the beginning of sorrows. This young girl, who'd been presumably sheltered and well-provided for by her family, was now virtually a fugitive. And she would be for her entire life, all because she'd said, "Yes" to God. Some believe she also lost the one thing any young woman in such a lonely, terrifying situation would eventually crave: the bond of precious sexuality in a marriage.

These losses, though not as dramatic or well-reported, were magnified as the boy grew. She had a first cruel taste of the wrenching separations to come when she and Joseph lost Jesus on the way home from a Passover celebration in Jerusalem. For three horrifying days she searched for her young son, no doubt berating herself for losing the one thing that had justified all her previous losses. Did she wonder if God was angry at her for not paying close enough attention? Can her guilt and self-recrimination even be imagined?

Still when she found him, his first comment revealed that she had already begun to lose him forever. His cool words to his frantic parents? "Why did you search for me? Did you not know I would be in my Father's house?" At that moment, with those words, the full weight of the beginning of utter loss and sorrow must have descended on Mary.

Before that final loss could be made complete, Mary's life was rocked by another massive loss. The mother who knew she would soon lose her son, first lost her husband. The man who had believed her claim of virginity. The man who had altered the course of his life—several times!—based on dreams and his love for her. The man who had protected her from both friend and foe. The man who had agreed to raise the Son of God. All for her sake. He died just a short time before Jesus would leave her to begin his ministry. It is likely she was still grieving for Joseph when Jesus resolutely left her to take up his mantle.

Once again, she lost any hope of home and stability. If she wanted to see her son, she had to go where he was. Yet she couldn't completely give up her home because he would need it as a base. Not to mention the fact that as soon as Jesus started "making headlines" she would be viewed by some with suspicion. Not everyone followed Jesus or even felt neutral about him. Indeed, those most powerful opposed him. Mary again found herself in a situation where whatever good reputation she'd surely established was suddenly thrust into question. Her theretofore quiet son was speaking out against all authority, socializing with thieves, beggars, foreigners, and prostitutes, and claiming to be the Son of God. What would the neighbors think?

All this would lead to the ultimate loss, the loss of the son for whom she'd given everything. Did she know what was coming? Did she wake every day of those three years during Jesus' ministry sick to her stomach with sorrow and fear? This final loss would not be quick. It would be long and slow and anguishing. Mary would see it coming at every turn. When Jesus threatened the Jewish leaders with provocative healings and proclamations. When Jesus violently cleared the temple of those who contributed to its revenue. When Jesus taunted Herod and ignored Pilate. When Jesus spun parables that condemned those in power. Finally, when Jesus virtually assured his own condemnation by first raising Lazarus from the dead and following this with the triumphant entry into Jerusalem through the gate that Scripture identified as the one the Messiah would use.

After all this came the scourgings, the crown of thorns, the cross.

Mary, queen of Christendom, revered by the Muslims, good Jewish girl—is the very embodiment of loss. How did Mary respond as every important part of her life was taken from her? Did she rail against these disasters at every juncture? Did she beg God for a change in the plan? Did she drag her feet, whine, complain, demand a different role and a different outcome?

What do we know of Mary's reaction to her losses? When God asked her to become pregnant in a culture where she could be stoned for it, she quietly agreed. When her family shamefacedly sent her away to her elder cousin in the hill country, she arrived singing the praises of God. When Joseph informed her that, despite the fact that she was nine months pregnant, she must make a difficult journey to Bethlehem, she packed her few possessions. When she was forced our of her country by Herod's wrath, she made a home for her husband and son in a foreign land.

When the child Jesus deliberately stayed behind in Jerusalem, causing his parents all kinds of trouble and fear, she merely kept his response in her heart and led him back home. When Joseph died and Jesus left to begin his ministry, leaving her alone for virtually the first time in her life, Mary not only refused to try to stop her son, she actually pushed him to begin his work. Scripture records her insisting that Jesus perform the water-to-wine miracle at the Cana wedding, even overruling his objection that it was not yet his time. That very miracle was the one that launched Jesus' ministry, and it was Mary who forced the moment.

At no point in Scripture—not when Jesus was becoming a prominent radical, not when he entered Jerusalem through the fated gate, not during the week of very public and revolutionary teachings and appearances, not when he said his disciples must eat his flesh and drink his blood, not when he allowed himself to be captured, beaten, betrayed, and crucified—is there any sign that Mary trying to stop him. She does not ask him to tone it down; she does not remind him that he is all she has; she does not protest, beg, cling, or even offer counsel. She just watches and waits.

Mary evinces a trust in God that is, even now all these years later with our "big picture" perspective, almost impossible to fathom.

We who struggle with our own losses may not have the capacity for trust demonstrated by Mary and Abraham, but we can take them as our models. Betty has spent her entire adult life striving for such a faith in the face of painful losses. Always a shy and out-of-place child, she—very much like Mary—did not fit into her world or community. A disability only made matters worse. She was, she says, "a classic loner. I was also partially deaf, which only served to set me apart from people even more and made me feel like a mis-fit." When she was dubbed "Most Bashful" by her high school class-mates, it was a label "I thought I'd carry to my grave, but fortunate-ly God had other plans for me."

Betty's life has been one long effort to trust to God's plan for her life. It has not always been easy in view of the many losses she's experienced. Worried she'd never marry, she finally met a man in graduate school who paid attention to her. She was thrilled when he asked her to marry him, perhaps too thrilled and desperate to fit in to see him for who he really was. Within a short time, he became mean, sarcastic, and physically and emotionally abusive. After tak-ing a job that forced her to leave her family and home state, he became even more cruel.

Betty, accustomed to thinking everything that was wrong was wrong with her, fell into the trap of believing his taunts and insults.

He made sure that all the unfamiliar "friends" within their new circle were his, leaving her isolated and rejected once again. When he began a relationship with a woman in this group, Betty feared the worst. But he dismissed her concerns, insulting her sanity and calling her a fool for being jealous in the process. "At this point, I really began to think I was crazy and hated myself for not trusting him," she recalls.

The loss of what fragile self-esteem she'd managed to build was complete and devastating. In a desperate cry for help, she began to steal from her employer. Although she'd hoped that her husband would see how much she needed his attention and affection, he had the opposite reaction when she was caught stealing. He viciously berated her, accusing her of being insane and of trying to ruin his life and career. In fact it was the perfect excuse for him to continue his affair and be rid of her once and for all. So, after losing her dignity, self-esteem, moral direction, job, and good standing in the law, Betty lost her marriage.

She readily acknowledges considering suicide. "I always tell people that I became a Christian in a McDonald's parking lot because that's where I landed while on my way to driving my car over the edge of one of the quarries," she says. "Even though I hadn't prayed to God in years, I decided to ask him…if God would somehow take me, this wretched person who had committed a criminal act and failed as a wife and ruined her life…and give me a second chance, I promised to try to change into the servant God intended me to be." All she could do then was trust.

Shortly afterward, her husband drove her half-way across the country, unceremoniously depositing her on her parents' doorstep. Before long the divorce was finalized. Slowly, she started to see God's work in what she'd considered the mess she'd made of her life. Although she cried through many long nights, her days began to offer some hope. She returned to school and was offered a job that forced her to be with people all the time. Indeed, the job required an assertive, self-confident presentation, and she accepted the position with some trepidation. It turned out to be one of the best decisions she ever made. Not only did the position provide her with a new start, it gave her a newfound sense of confidence. She also joined a new church, filled with people who understood her losses as well as her desire to put her trust fully in God.

Then, as often happens when we start to recover, another devastating strike stopped her cold. Her mother, the one who'd welcomed her back home after so many losses and disasters, died while on vacation with her father in Italy. The circumstances made the situation even more distressing. Betty remembers, "It took over ten days to get the Italian Embassy to release her body. The saddest day of my life was the day I had to go to Kennedy Airport and watch my dad come through the international arrival gate pushing my mom's empty suitcases."

She felt like she'd been hurled back to those darker days, unsure she could cope with this new, unexpected, and massive loss. But instead of falling back into the desperation and chaos of the past, she relied on what she'd learned about God's faithfulness and her own faith. "I felt suddenly thrown back into that same lost state I was in the year before when I got divorced," she says. "Having a parent die made me feel vulnerable and alone in the world. I knew at that point that I could do one of two things: I could allow the loneliness and depression to consume me and regress back to the person I was before God began to open me up, or I could take the joy that my mom gave me and try to pass it on. I decided to say thank you to God for the gift of my mother."

She made her grieving process into a commitment to reach out more to people in her church and others who needed support. She began attending more programs through her church, often finding herself inspired by various speakers as well as by other members of her congregation. These experiences lent her the courage to start teaching Sunday School, a responsibility she found to be as wonderful for her as it was for her students. She expanded her involvement with young people by teaching at a Vacation Bible School and volunteering as a camp counselor.

But it was only when a co-worker was going through a miserable divorce that Betty realized just how much her losses had taught her, and how capably she could use them to help others. After connecting with the woman, Betty realized "how God has been working on me my entire life to help me see things that were previously unclear. At that moment, I really knew that using the wounds of my life to reach out and soothe the wounds of someone else is what all the struggle is about."

She's also discovered that the key to weathering life's repeated strikes is to stop trying to predict and control every outcome. It is also a matter of learning to forgive ourselves and accept that we are merely human. She explains, "As I stumble along in my walk with God, I've learned that God will work out his plan no matter how we mess up or try to manipulate the situation. We won't be happy or at peace with God's will for us if we're trying to control things. I've found the most peace when I've managed to let go and trust God."

So did Abraham. So did Mary. So can we.

TALKING IT OVER WITH GOD

Lord, in those dark moments during the middle of the night, I lay awake thinking of how much I have to lose. And it terrifies me! I thought I had a lot to lose the last time, and I did lose more than I thought possible then. I wasn't sure I'd be able to survive that. How then can I possibly live with the prospect of my loss this time?

I am sabotaged by the feeling that everything that's precious to me—not to mention everything I need to survive—is up for grabs, about to disappear. I'm petrified that those things I most need to successfully fight this new battle are slipping from my grasp. My sanity. My health. My family. My work. My confidence. And sometimes, God help me, my faith.

Lord, reach out to calm my fears! Remind me of Paul's repeated declaration that all is mere loss in comparison to what is gained in God. Restore my faith! Cradle me in your reassuring arms as I mourn. Whisper hope into my ear. Open my mind—which is clenched shut against the dread of loss—to your abundant presence. Release me from my fear, Lord, free me from the specter of grief so that I may see what you would have me gain.

ASK YOURSELF

1. Have you ever been so disturbed about your losses that you've failed to consider your gains?

2. When you think about others who are troubled, do you tend to believe that their pain is not nearly as searing and debilitating as yours?

3. Can you see any "blessings" in your sorrows?

TAKING FURTHER ACTION

• Recite or read Psalm 23, which has become a popular prayer for those in need: "The Lord is my shepherd...."

• Read Genesis, chapters 15, 18, and 22, which detail God's general promise to Abraham that he will be the father of nations, God's specific promise to Abraham and Sarah of the son to be born within the year, and the near-sacrifice and subsequent saving of Isaac.

• In a very real sense, every second (or third or fourth) strike represents a freshly painful new loss. Identify the fresh losses you've experienced when trouble has re-entered your life. They may include loss of health, loss of faith, loss of optimism, loss of energy.

Now consider the aftermath, the time during which you recovered. During that period and/or in the interim did you gain anything as a result of your initial crisis? Consider this carefully before rejecting it out of hand. Did you gain a friend or a new circle of friends? A greater understanding of your spouse and family? A deeper reliance on, and better relationship with, God—at least during that period? A new way to pray? Self-knowledge? Coping mechanisms? Support systems and groups? Now consider how those gains can help you in your current situation.

CHAPTER EIGHT

OR GAIN?

Someone came from the leader's house to say, "Your daughter is dead; do not trouble the teacher anymore." When Jesus heard this, he replied, "Do not fear. Only believe and she will be saved."

Luke 8:49–50

Jarius's heart must have broken when he heard the pronouncement that his beloved only daughter had died before he could bring Jesus to cure her. His devastating loss was made so much worse by the self-recriminating sense of failure he must have felt. Yet, just at the moment when he was ready to sink to the ground in despair, Jesus assures him that his daughter will live if only he believes.

Was Jarius able to believe? Are those of us who suffer today from painful losses able to believe Jesus' promise that we will experience salvation; that death will become life; that grieving will become laughing; that losses will indeed become gains?

To nurture and maintain such a belief in the face of repeated loss is extremely difficult. For some, at least initially, it may be impossible. Kathryn, the woman who lost her son and husband within months of each other, could not at first believe that anything good could ever come into her life again. "I was just drained of all hope," she says. "How could I go on with any sort of faith when the people I loved and depended upon so completely had been taken from me? That's the way I looked at it for quite a while: that they had been taken from me, as though I had been violated and robbed. With that kind of feeling, what room was there for hope, never mind the thought of gain?"

But something a minister said at her husband's funeral stayed with her, although she wasn't able to consciously acknowledge it for some time. He talked about seeing clearly through sorrow, seeing clearly enough to know that while we may experience excruciating loss at the death of a loved one, that person is experiencing extraordinary gain. They have joined God, and there is no greater gain than that. Though she heard him that day, Kathryn swiftly rejected his words. "At a time of such deep grief, the last thing I wanted to hear was that the ones I'd lost had attained the ultimate joy," she admits, now with a small smile. "It was just too hard to hear that. It gave me the image of them happily cavorting around heaven while I was in such agony. I really resented that minister! But you know, he was probably right. And eventually that became a tremendous comfort to me. After all, how long could I drag around in utter misery if they truly were happy?"

During the time of fresh grief, it is surely difficult to remember that death means life for the one who has gone to God. Because for those who mourn, death simply means death, an ending to all that has gone before and a bleak, sometimes unimaginable future. To believe that death means a beginning for the beloved one can seem impossible. Yet that's exactly what faith requires of us: to acknowledge through our sorrow and every other complex emotion that accompanies loss, that death is only a portal.

Isn't that the hard, shining truth that informed Mary's life? Every one of her repeated losses was repaid a thousand-fold when she saw her son alive and ready to embrace her on that blessed third day. And while those who experience such losses today may have to wait a little longer to be so magnificently reunited, the promise of that day remains. It is indeed the very core of our faith.

Ruby, after experiencing losses and gains for over eight decades, has learned to embrace this tenet of faith. A Christian realist who has scrupulously prepared for her own death, she also acknowledges with a chuckle, "I do want to go to God, because I do believe we will go to God.... I just don't necessarily want to go right now!" Then she adds in a musing tone, "I don't know why we're so afraid. We shouldn't be if we truly believe what we say we believe. Death is just the way to God."

She has held onto this belief despite recurring strikes as one member of her family—biological and adopted—after another has died. Raised on a farm with her parents and blind brother, she cared for her father at home until he died there shortly after her mother, who Ruby also managed to keep in the family home until just a few weeks before her death from cancer. "It was a blow when I lost my parents, especially my mother to cancer," she says. "But I was happy for them, that they would have no more suffering, that they were together again after such a short time apart. I told myself they had gone to God, and it would be selfish of me to want them back."

And selfish she is most certainly not. After the deaths of her parents, she cared for and protected her brother, keeping him safely in the home he'd been familiar with for his entire life. While he was still living, though doing poorly, she welcomed a friend who was very ill—also with cancer—into their home. "We really lived here in this house like three old family members," she recalls, not mentioning the strain it must have put on her to care for a blind, aging brother and a dying friend. "It all worked out. We never really got on each other's nerves. It's good for people to be at home for as long as they can." Like their father, her brother died there; she was fixing his lunch when he "went on to God."

Within too short a time, her good friend died. Even with grief upon grief, Ruby never relinquished her trust in God or her belief that her loss was their gain. And perhaps because of that quiet, relentless faith, she made some extraordinary gains herself. She didn't have to wonder for long whether she would be able to "be at home for as long as possible." The friend who had come to live and die in Ruby's old farmhouse had a son who built an addition onto the house after his mother moved in. He wanted to be close enough to help out with his mother whenever possible. When she died, he and his young family stayed. Grateful for all Ruby had done for his mother and drawn to her gentle kindness, he and his family have become hers.

So the woman who was so busy caring for others that she never married or had children of her own has a built-in family that is probably more committed to caring for her than most "real" sons and daughters. She is frequently delighted by the two little boys who race across the breezeway that connects the two houses to spend a few moments chatting with her. They open their Christmas presents with her on Christmas morning, and their mother sets up a tree in Ruby's parlor each December. She is invited to every family occasion or holiday, and she is kept young at heart by observing the antics of her two young neighbors and their cousins. When the heat goes on the fritz, when she has a doctor's appointment, when she needs someone to clean off the cobwebs she can barely see anymore, when she needs to go the grocery store, Ruby only has to ask.

If only all losses-turned-to-gains were so wonderfully evident. Those experiencing second strikes that do not necessarily involve death can struggle just as mightily with the notion that their losses will be turned to gains. In fact, these "living second strikes" can be even harder to negotiate because there is no long-held faith about moving on to a peaceful place with God. Those of us experiencing living second strikes are stuck right here trying to cope against incredible odds. Too often, we're afraid to even turn to God for help, forgetting that it is always there regardless of whether we consider ourselves worthy.

Robert knows just how difficult this can be. An alcoholic who has been sober for nearly four years, he is nonetheless still tortured by his second collapse into addiction, a decade after he first became sober. "Fourteen years ago, I hit bottom for the first time. I was certain it would be my last," admits Robert. "I was thirty-five years old at the time, and I'd all but blown my marriage, my job, my life, on alcohol. My 'bottom' happened one night when I drove off the road and into a power pole after stopping for a couple of drinks with the guys. Well, that couple of drinks went on for six hours, and when the cops found me it was after 1:00 AM. When I hit the pole I knocked power out for a couple of neighborhoods, and the whole story made the state's daily paper, complete with a photo of me with my head gashed, looking so drunk it was just pathetic.

"Humiliated is not nearly a strong enough word to describe how I felt. Within a week, I'd been harassed by reporters, my wife had taken our three- and five-year-old daughters and had moved out, and I was facing a criminal trial for DUI, not to mention the local electric company which was trying to recover costs for the damage I'd done. My reaction was to hole up in the house and drink more. But I was lucky: I had one person who was not going to let me kill myself. My boss was a recovering alcoholic himself, and he basically pushed his way into the house, sat me down, and laid it out. If I wanted to die, there was nothing he could do about it, he said. But if I was ready to admit I needed help, he would get the company to pay for rehab. It was just that simple. I was ready."

Robert survived the rehab center, eventually leaving the program and attending daily Alcoholic Anonymous meetings. His boss, who'd held his job open for him, became his sponsor. Slowly he put his life back together. His wife, who began to go to Al-Anon, agreed to marriage counseling. Though he knew he could not undo the damage he'd done to his young daughters, he gradually began to win his daughters' trust back.

"I can remember one day when I had to leave the room because

I started crying," he says, his voice raw with the memory. "We were playing with Legos, and I'd made them laugh with the silly things I was building. We were just having a really great time. Then, my oldest, all of six at the time, turned to me and asked, 'Are you going to stay the 'good Daddy?' Apparently the girls had taken to calling me the good Daddy' when I was around and sober, and the 'bad Daddy' when I was drunk. You know when people say they can feel their heart breaking? Well, it's true. I believed that moment alone would keep me sober for the rest of my life and beyond."

He was wrong. Robert's second strike came nearly ten years later when a co-worker told him that his wife was involved with another man. He blamed himself, remembering what he'd put her through and knowing she'd never completely recovered or regained her trust in him. He was unable to feel the least bit of anger toward her, focusing it all on himself. Finally, he gently confronted her, taking all the blame himself and telling her the he'd be willing to resume the marriage counseling they'd ended a few years before.

"She just looked at me and said, 'No.' That was it. No maybe. No explanation. Not even a denial." Robert says. "I felt like such an idiot. Here I'd thought I was being such a good, patient husband, taking it all on myself and offering to go to marriage counseling...like I was willing to do her this huge favor. I was all ready for the next step of saving our marriage, while all the time she had no intention of saving it. It was already lost to her.

"I went out that night and got well and truly trashed."

He stayed that way for over a month, thus allowing his wife to make a good case for obtaining sole custody of their now teenage daughters. Those weeks became a vicious cycle: the more bad news he got—his wife's suit for divorce, her intention to gain custody, reported sightings of her and the girls on public outings with the other man—the more Robert drank.

"When I most needed not to drink is when I drank the most," he says softly, shaking his head. "When I most needed to be fighting for my life with all my faculties, I could barely lift my face out of the scotch glass. I can't explain, and it still scares me to think about how easily I gave in after ten years. And though I'm not proud to say this, it was not easy to see God in any of what was happening to me. The idea that losses as severe as mine could ever be turned to anything good seemed just plain ridiculous. I just couldn't get there."

It was, once again, his wise and experienced boss, James, who got him there. AA sponsors take their responsibilities very seriously, and James never gave up on Robert. Eventually, James made him see that this relapse did not have to be permanent, but that unless he got a grip on himself, he would lose any prospect of seeing his daughters or recovering his life. Back in rehab, Robert worked hard on reaching out to God, his Higher Power, and taking responsibility for himself. He also learned what not to take responsibility for.

"I knew, as soon as I started to tentatively pray again, that God was right there; that he'd never left me at all," he says, "and I knew that God had already forgiven me. I actually felt that forgiveness flow over me. I also felt God showing me that I was not to blame for all the problems in the world—or even in my poor life. I'd always been secretly skeptical about people who say God talks to them. No more! The message I received then was, 'Don't be so arrogant, Robert. You didn't make the world; you didn't even make your little part of it, so don't presume that everything that goes right— or wrong—is your responsibility. The world does not revolve around you!' I don't know which made me feel more relieved: the forgiveness or this idea that everything wasn't always my fault."

Robert was sober long enough before the divorce was final to successfully petition for partial custody of his daughters. Although they were hurt by his relapse and deeply influenced by their mother's resentment and disappointment, they had not forgotten the ten years with the "good Daddy." They gradually allowed him back into their lives. Recently, he chauffeured his older daughter on the seven-hour drive to begin her sophomore year at college. He's helping his youngest work on her college applications.

Are these gains big and dramatic enough to make up for his losses?

"I don't look at it in that way," he explains. "Fourteen years ago, and then again four years ago, I never thought my life would be worth anything. From that perspective, are these wonderful and amazing gains? You bet. Do I think God's through shaping me yet? No. We're taking it one day at a time."

TALKING IT OVER WITH GOD

Lord, I just don't know if I'm strong enough to see the opportunities for gain in the midst of this maelstrom. I don't know if I can be like Jarius, who managed to believe against all odds. Have mercy on me, Lord! Help my unbelief!

Show me the gains that have come into my life after past crises. Remind me of all the good that has come of pain in my life and the lives of others. Open my mind to the gains that have come from losses throughout history: the Great Depression resulting in social and employment programs; the horror of racism leading to the civil rights legislation; a deadly earthquake in Iran allowing nations to lay down political arms and lend help.

Lord, help me to remember that you are the only One who turns loss into gain. Let me strive to be like Jarius and Mary, the sister of Lazarus, and all those who earnestly said, "Yes, Lord," when you asked them to believe. Most of all, let me take as my model, Mary, your own mother, who experienced sorrow after sorrow after sorrow, and yet still held onto the hope that the gain would come. As it did. Above all, Lord, let my ultimate hope for gain be hers: the Resurrection.

ASK YOURSELF

1. Do you believe that with faith your losses can somehow become gains?

2. If you have lost a loved one, do you believe that the person has passed into salvation with God and that you will be reunited?

3. Have you ever been surprised at how the loss of something material, like a job or investment, can in the end lead to a gain?

TAKING FURTHER ACTION

• Watch the movie *Men of Honor* and observe how the two main characters, Robert DiNero and Cuba Gooding, Jr., work in different ways to turn their individual losses into gains.

• Read Luke, chapter 8, and focus on how the various people who come to Jesus for help with their losses utterly trust him to turn them into gains.

• Consider a specific loss you are now struggling with. It may be the loss of someone you love; it may be the loss of income; it may be the loss of faith. Try, for the moment, to put aside your disappointment, sorrow, mourning, anger, fear, and even bitterness. You will probably not be able to banish these emotions for very long, but try to ignore their impact for this short time.

Imagine you are someone else observing your loss. From that perspective, make a list of all the possible ways your loss might some day become a gain. Post this list where you will see it every day, and read it whenever you feel overwhelmed and uncertain that you will recover. Eventually, select one hoped-for outcome that makes you most comfortable, and begin, at your own pace, to do what is necessary to pursue it.

CHAPTER NINE:

BABY STEPS
ON THE JOURNEY

Jesus answered him, "Very truly, I tell you, no one can see the kingdom of God without being born from above." John 3:3

When Jesus insists that one must be born again to experience the kingdom of God, Nicodemus is, understandably, astonished. Is Jesus suggesting that we literally lose this life to gain another, unknown existence? How can one crawl into the womb and be born again, Nicodemus asks.

As well he might. Those who have chosen rebirth as a result of multiple sorrows can attest that it is no easy commitment, or process, for that matter. Rebirth requires a willing decision to embrace the loss of all that is familiar in the confident belief of a greater gain. In fact, the pain and mess of the first birth, human birth, is nothing compared to what it takes to be born again. This second birth is so much more difficult because the person being born again must be both mother and infant, experiencing the pain, fear, and uncertainty of both. And while pregnant mothers are relatively young and hearty, those of us seeking to be born again often carry the emotional and physical aches of a lifetime.

Violet's rebirth has just begun, even as she approaches her fifty-ninth birthday. A lifetime of multiple strikes caused mostly by abusive relationships made her yearn for a new life. When her second husband died of an alcohol-related liver ailment five years ago, she decided she could either fold up and spend her golden years in darkness, or she could examine her past and present to ensure a new future. The choice may seem simple, a literal no-brainer. It wasn't.

"When you've been abused all your life, it's not easy to be kind to yourself," explains Violet, who tends to refer to "my old self" as you and her newly born self as I. "And it's even harder to reach down and find the energy, or let's face it, the guts, to try to find a new way. You have no self-confidence. You have physical scars and continual pain from the beatings you've taken. And that doesn't even touch on the mental pain. You really just want to lay down, watch TV, and rest until it's all over. You truly do. It's not pretty to say that, but it's the truth."

The first abuse Violet experienced was relatively subtle, but it established the pattern that would mar her life. Her mother was a frustrated, angry woman who would most certainly have pursued a career today. But despite the fact that she was a notable student and avid reader, working class girls just didn't go to college in those days. So when at the age of nineteen she became pregnant with Violet's older brother, she gave up the dream of college and a life different from what she considered her own mother's miserable existence. Completely succumbing to the times and the demands of her parents, she married her unborn baby's father, a charming high school drop-out who worked on a commercial fishing boat. Violet believes that, despite this unpromising start, her parents did love each other, at least initially.

"My mother would show off the wedding photos, pasted in a

cheap, white dime-store album, with the edges of the pictures all jagged and fading," Violet remembers. "She was dressed in white—her mother had insisted—and she wasn't showing with my brother yet, so the wedding must have happened right away. She and my father actually look happy in a few of the pictures, though in those days, most wedding photos were pretty solemn. From the pictures, you really can't tell what my mother was thinking. You never could."

Violet does know that her mother loved the baby boy who came of that shotgun wedding. Her brother, George, was the clear favorite and her mother made no attempt to hide it. Instead, she used her devotion to George as a weapon against Violet almost from the moment she was born eighteen months after the marriage. That the weapon was invisible did not make it any less dangerous. Indeed, the fact that it could not be seen, and therefore identified or confronted, made it all the more damaging. Violet explains, "You never understood, really, that my mother hated you because she never said that outright. You just knew how very much she loved my brother. And there was nothing you could do about that. It's not like you could accuse her of loving him, when what you really wanted to do is scream, 'Why do you hate me?'"

Violet was too young to comprehend the reasons for her mother's resentment. Indeed, decades before counseling, Donahue, and Oprah were woven into the fabric of our culture, Violet's mother probably didn't fully understand her own motives. Though she may not have intended to do the damage she did, she became increasingly manipulative, making Violet her victim. By the time Violet reached puberty, her mother's abuse was an integral part of the girl's life. Some days, it passed from emotional battering to physical assaults. Her mother burned her with cigarettes, chopped off her long hair as a punishment for lying, and even slapped her on one of the rare occasions Violet brought a couple of schoolmates home.

"It was so humiliating you'd never dare bring friends home again," Violet says. "Not that there were many to begin with. When you had that kind of treatment at home, in a small town, everyone knew about it. The other kids would make fun; they didn't want to hang out with you. Their parents didn't want them around you or your family, anyway. Of course, George's friends were always welcome, and he could go to other kids' houses whenever he wanted. He could do no wrong in her eyes. And though I guess, looking back, that he might have wanted to help, he didn't know how. Besides, why would he risk making her mad at him, too?"

Violet's father was simply not around. As soon as he realized he was becoming the primary target of his wife's resentment, he began to absent himself from the home. His job provided the perfect excuse; commercial fisherman often work long and unpredictable hours. The more he was gone, the more enraged and disgusted his wife became. Violet says of her father, "He wasn't a bad guy at all. Just timid. Here he was, this big rugged guy, and he couldn't stand up to her. Ever. That's how vicious she could be. Whether he was there or not, all she'd do is put him down; it was enough to make you fantasize that he'd just hit her. Beat her until she shut up. You'd just sort of think about that happening, and how it would be understandable for him to do it."

So Violet wasn't all that surprised when it began to happen to her in her first marriage. By the time she met her future husband, she was accustomed to violence from the one person who was supposed to love her the most. She thinks now that in a perverse way, she was even attracted to that sort of treatment. Abuse had come to represent love to her. When she started dating the young man who would become her husband in just four short months, she knew of his reputation for a quick temper. Her friends tried to warn her, even pointing out that he'd spent a night or two in the local jail, cooling off after a fight, though he'd never been formally charged with assault. He usually charmed his way out of trouble, another aspect of his personality that seduced Violet.

But what really attracted her to him was how much her mother hated him. She would rail at Violent, telling her how stupid she was to "fall for low-class scum like that!" She'd sneer at her daughter for allowing herself to be blinded by his good looks and machismo, calling him an "uneducated, unemployed moron." The more her mother harangued, the more Violet preened about her boyfriend, using him to aggravate her mother every chance she got. Not only would he be her ticket out of her parent's house, he was the first act of true and complete disobedience that her mother couldn't punish her for.

When she became pregnant at twenty, she was almost jubilant. Boasting to his buddies that he knew he'd fathered a son, her boyfriend immediately agreed to "do the right thing," as he put it, never once mentioning love; they were married ten days later. Violet recalls, "It was all about getting out of that house. And the fact that she hated him so much made it even better when she found out about the pregnancy." She pauses for a slow, sad smile before adding, "You never once let yourself think that in trying to pay her back, you were walking into the same trap she'd fallen into." The only thing Violet remembers about her wedding day was trying to ignore the sadness in her silent father's eyes.

The verbal abuse began immediately; he waited until after the baby was born to start hitting her. He used the fact that she'd borne a daughter, something he considered a failure that would embarrass him in front of his buddies, against her. He raged at Violent, claiming that he was meant to have sons. His father had had only sons, and so had his grandfather. She was the weak link, he yelled at first; then, coming home drunk one night, he changed his tune. The baby was not his at all, he snarled at her, she was a slut who slept with some wimp and then tricked him into marrying her and now expected him to raise a bastard. When she denied his accusation with horrified, though not yet frightened, tears, he hit her. It was just once that first time, and though he never apologized, he did quiet down for a while.

Unfortunately, their daughter was colicky, and he couldn't take all the crying. Again he blamed Violet, renewing his accusation and coming home drunk several times a week. "In those days—in that town—it was expected that a man would drink some. That's what the guys did, and no wife would tell her husband to stop. Of course, most husbands knew when to stop, and even if they didn't, they wouldn't come home and throw their wife down the stairs," Violet says quietly. "But when you're used to taking the blame for everything, it doesn't occur to you that he might be the one who is wrong. You're used to thinking it's your fault."

Which, she thinks, is why she stayed with him for almost a decade. She couldn't turn to her family, though they lived only a few towns away. Her mother had heard about her situation and taunted Violet at every chance, raising the childish refrain, "I told you so," to a cruel art form. George had long since moved across the country to the West Coast, having as little contact with his family as possible and making their mother all the more bitter. Violet's father would help out in the only way he knew how, by giving her what cash he could spare without her mother finding out. The fighting spirit he would have needed to help his daughter in a more substantive way had been long since leeched out of him.

She might have stayed past their tenth anniversary, had he not hit their daughter. It was over a small thing that Violet can no longer remember, and she says now, "It was probably a miracle that it hadn't happened sooner, but it was still so unexpected. When it happened, you were just in shock. That sounds stupid, but it's true. When the shock finally wore off, all you could think about was getting her out of there, not putting her through what you'd been through."

To her surprise, George sent money and the name of a good attorney, who didn't bother seeking alimony since her husband was too shiftless to hold a real job. But he earned his fee tenfold by making certain that all possible restraining orders were entered and by letting the local cops—the same ones who'd brought her husband home drunk countless nights despite knowing what he'd likely do to her once inside—know that if she wasn't protected, their miserable little police force would be national news—after he'd sued them and the town into oblivion.

When the divorce was final, the good attorney handed Violet a check for ten thousand dollars, assuring her George had paid his fees and wanted this to be given to her "to start a new life." She and her daughter left for Boston. She recalls crying on the train for the first time since she married because she didn't even have an address for her brother. She couldn't even thank him. And she knew, remembering their childhood, that that's the way he wanted it.

Violet isn't sure whether it was George's unexpected kindness or the lawyer's respectful treatment, but she managed to find enough confidence to at least start a new life in a town just south of Boston. She enrolled her daughter in school, applied for and—to her amazement—got a job in the school's cafeteria so that she could be home when her daughter was, and spent weekends trying to get their tiny apartment clean and in order. She wanted to let her father know where she was, that she was doing OK, but she wouldn't risk her mother discovering anything about her new life. "You know, you're sort of convinced, even that far away, that she can still poison everything," Violet says. "Of course, you can also make the mistake of going so far in the opposite direction—trying to get away from everything that's been wrong—that you end up at the same starting point, feeling just as stupid."

And that, she now knows, is exactly what she did. Rather than try to discover what she wanted out of a new life, she simply gravitated to anything that was the opposite of what she'd known. She went overboard: not only did she steer clear of aggressive or working class men, she wouldn't date anyone; instead of disciplining her daughter in a careful, loving way, she refused to discipline her at all in order to avoid making her daughter hate her the way she'd hated her mother; rather than speaking up when she deserved a raise or promotion at work, she said nothing to keep from sounding like her mother, who complained about everything. For nearly nine years, she lived like a quiet hermit, making few friends and focusing all her energy on her daughter. When the girl left for college, Violet had to face how empty her life had become. At forty, she was completely alone, with a dead-end job and a daughter who resented her smothering brand of love.

"In that kind of situation, with that kind of depression," she explains, "you sort of panic about life. You become willing to take the first thing that comes along."

At first glance, that "first thing"—the president of the local bank where she'd kept an account and applied for loans for her daughter's college—looked good, especially because he appeared to be the absolute opposite of everything she'd known in her first marriage. He was successful, intelligent, educated, well-respected; and as much as Violet couldn't believe it, attracted to her. Though she'd shyly avoided his advances in the past, now that her daughter was gone, Violet finally gave in. Suddenly caught up in what could be called a whirlwind romance, she found herself dining at fine restaurants, meeting a class of people she'd never known before, and accepting elegant gifts. Overwhelmed by the kind of attention she'd never imagined receiving, she managed to overlook his tendencies to correct her speech, buy her "appropriate" clothes, and tell her what books to read. She also ignored his consumption of scotch.

"You just don't want to think about those things when the other things seem so good and exciting," she explains. "For the first time in your life, you're being treated like a queen. Why argue?"

Nor did she argue when he told her they would be married. When he gave her the conservative suit dress he'd bought for the wedding, told her it was scheduled for a weekend her daughter would be taking college exams, and presented her with the wedding bands he'd already selected, she meekly acquiesced. She didn't mention that he'd never actually asked her to marry him, that she wanted to have her daughter present, that the entire guest list comprised his friends and family. She also didn't tell him how uncomfortable his grown children from a previous marriage made her feel with their ill-concealed disdain. Within a year of their marriage, his bank was acquired and he was offered a promotion, providing he was willing to move to Tennessee. He agreed without consulting her. She packed dutifully.

The new position brought with it a lovely, southern home, a built-in set of new upper-class friends, and more pressure than her husband had ever experienced. He dealt with it by drinking more scotch, not to mention entire bottles of wine at dinner, and by turning his frustration on Violet. The "makeover" that had started with correcting her language and choosing her clothes accelerated into ridiculing her in public and virtually ignoring her in private. Though he never hit her, Violet realizes now that she made the same mistake in her second marriage she'd made in her first: running away from the past rather than toward the future. She chose her first husband to both escape and get revenge on her mother; she chose her second because he appeared to be the opposite of her first. "You think you've learned something," she declares with regret, "but you really haven't. It seems like you do everything the hard way."

The pattern of her first marriage repeated herself. Her husband's cruelty eroded whatever self-confidence she had left; she felt unable to defend herself or leave. But though she'd dreaded the move to Tennessee, it turned out to be her salvation. Seeking some sort of solace, she began attending a small local church. Though she never spoke herself or attempted to reach out to anyone—indeed she confesses that she barely raised her eyes to meet the gaze of those who spoke to her—she felt immediately welcome. She heard people crying out and praising aloud in church; many talked about being saved or reborn. Though she'd been raised to be suspicious of such behavior, she felt warm and safe among these church-goers. She even managed to resist her husband's scornful insistence that she not be seen attending "that place."

What comfort she received over the next several years came through "that place." And when her husband, who'd heaped disdain upon her church friends, became severely ill with liver disease, those very church friends were the ones who helped her care for him. "He may not have liked them helping," Violet says with a small smile, "but by then he was too weak to do anything about it." By the time he died after nearly two years of suffering, she'd been purged of her fear and awe of him. She also had more time to devote to her church. The day she buried him, she says, is the day she began to be born again.

"I don't think I can say I am born again the way my friends at church describe it," she explains. "Most of them can recite the time and day and year that they were reborn. They relate the experience in great detail, as if it was a revelation with thunder and lightning and the whole show. That didn't happen to me. My 'birthing process,' if that's the right term, has been slower and maybe harder. Sometimes I wish I could be bonked on the head with a revelation and know exactly how God has chosen me and what he wants of me! I think that would be easier.

"For me, it's been baby steps. Moving away from the fear of my husband. Forgiving him enough to nurse him. Spending more time at church. Getting baptized. Starting therapy at fifty-five—and then not quitting when I discovered I should have had it at fifteen! Having people over to the house for a meal. Even just thinking of the house as mine. All these have been small steps in being born again. I'm learning that this birth is as painful—and as joyful—as an actual birth. Having my daughter was nothing compared to this!

"Some of my church friends believe I have to have the whole experience—the bonking on the head sort of thing—or it's not real. I think they feel I'm not really saved unless I'm saved in the way they understand. But I've spent my whole life trying to do what others think I should. I'm not doing that anymore.

"I think God is saving me every day, a little bit at a time."

TALKING IT OVER WITH GOD

Lord, do I have what it takes to be born again, to become like a child? Do I have the innocence? Can I possess such newness of soul? Have I the courage to be completely dependent on you? Can I become pure enough? Am I both strong and weak enough?

Can I cleanse my mind of "old ways?" Will I clear my mind of doubts and let you fill it with hope? Do I have the ability to trust so completely? Can I simply cry out for help when I'm hungry or tired or lonely or needy, instead of repressing all in the name of so-called strength? Will I laugh ever again with sweet abandon when something entertains me?

Might I run toward you and throw myself into your waiting arms? Can I allow myself to climb into your lap and snuggle in your arms? Will I listen to your whispered words of love and comfort? Am I going to be able to relax in the sound of your peaceful silence? Will I take tiny steps in the direction you lead me? Can I dance and rejoice merely because I am in your presence? Can I? Will I? Might I? I will. I must.

ASK YOURSELF

1. What is your first reaction when someone tells you they've been "born again" or "saved"?

2. Have you ever yearned for the chance to be born again, to start all over again?

3. Do you believe that by being "born from above," as Jesus describes it, you might become closer to God and more able to trust him as you address your troubles?

TAKING FURTHER ACTION

• Read Charles Dickens' *A Christmas Carol*, paying particular attention to how long Scrooge suffers before he embraces the chance to be born again. Also, be sure to note how "baby-like" and uncoordinated Scrooge is as and after he is reborn.

• Read John, chapter 3, for a full discussion of what Jesus means by "born again."

• When you awaken tomorrow morning, be "born again." Experience every part of your day, from washing your face in the morning to brushing your teeth before bed, as though it was completely new to you. Approach each event of your day with innocence as if you'd never known it before. Concentrate. Do you like a little or a lot of milk in your cereal? How do you really feel when your teenager ignores you? When your toddler puts his warm little arms around your neck? When your boss praises you? When a colleague acts enviously? When you don't feel like cooking? When your spouse is late for dinner?

Now think of how you can respond differently according to how the "reborn" you feels about these details. If you are hurt by your teenager, could you simply tell her? If you are comforted by your toddler, could you hold him a few moments longer? If you don't feel like cooking, could you make sandwiches or order takeout? Some things will be easier than others. You can have more milk in your cereal without upsetting anyone; you probably cannot address your spouse's tardiness without upsetting something. Remember that being born again is not easy! Now take the lessons you've learned in these every day matters and apply them to the more difficult challenges in your life.

CHAPTER TEN

NEW HORIZONS

He waited another seven days, and again, he sent out the dove from the ark; and the dove came back to him in the evening, and there in its beak was a freshly plucked olive leaf; so Noah knew that the waters had subsided from the earth. Genesis 8:10–11

For those reading the story of Noah and the ark, this is a relatively anticlimactic moment. After all, they've already seen the wild deluge pour upon the earth and the annihilating flood cover even the highest mountain. So how exciting, really, is the return of a dove with an olive leaf in its mouth?

But to Noah, it was the moment he'd been waiting for; the moment when a new horizon materialized.

Like Noah, for those bearing the burden of a second strike, that breathtaking moment when a new horizon appears, against all odds, is both wondrous and frightening. Because, make no mistake, Noah was as frightened as he was exhilarated. As with all who have yearned for an end to sorrows, the new horizon represents the frightening unknown as well as the chance for a new life. One moment we're like newborns, barely ready for baby steps, and the next we have a stunning vision of where those steps may lead.

This is a particularly overwhelming moment for those struggling with illness. Most nurses and caregivers are very familiar with the mini-crisis that ensues when a patient's initial pain and terror subsides, giving way to both anticipation and fear of what comes next.

Debbie, a nurse at a long-term health care facility describes it. "When they come in, they might be in terrible pain, they might be heavily medicated, they might be in shock. So they tend to be very docile, accepting, just wanting to get through it. But as soon as they start feeling a little better, as soon as the pain or terror recedes a bit, there's a whole new set of worries: When will I get out of here? Will I be able to manage at home? Will I need help? Will I be able to *get* help? How much will all this cost? What about my job? My spouse? My kids? What it all boils down to at this point is, What does the future hold?"

It's the question lurking in the back of all our minds, but it is most pressing for those of us who find ourselves slowly recovering from a second strike. Just when everyone assumes we should be happily relieved about the prospect of a new horizon, we're most likely to be floored by a potent mixture of fear and joy. And relief may be the farthest thing from our mind.

Experiencing this myself, I've done enough informal research to know it is a tendency that I share with many cancer survivors. When I go for my regular skin check appointments, I can expect one of two initial outcomes: a biopsy, or not. In the case of a biopsy, my doctor is removing something that may have changed or that he's been watching for some time or that he thinks may, at some time, develop into a melanoma. No biopsy means he's not concerned about anything right now. Choosing which outcome I'd prefer should be a no-brainer, right?

Well, not exactly. When my doctor does a biopsy, I feel that a disaster may have been prevented. I don't enjoy being cut, I resent the scars, I am usually anxious for much of the seven to fourteen days it may take to get the report. But in the end, I know. I know what secrets that patch of skin held, and I know that danger has been eradicated. Besides, after countless biopsies, I've learned to expect good news. And I believe that the patch that has been removed is no longer even a potential problem for me.

With no biopsy, I leave the doctor's office feeling schizophrenic, even a little deflated. After all, I'd spent the past several days steeling myself for this appointment, for the possibility of a biopsy. And then there's none. Yes, I'm happy not to be cut, not to have to wait two weeks, not to have the bandages and the new scar to contend with. But in the back of my mind are those two little words: right now. Nothing has to be removed *right now*. There doesn't appear to be a new cancer right now. Before my second strike, I spent six years basking in the belief that there was no cancer right now. Then I learned that right now doesn't mean forever. So I'm not quite as enamored these days of right now.

I feel like a bit of an idiot when my husband, family, and friends rejoice over no biopsy. Don't they fully comprehend the meaning of right now? Well, no, they don't, not in the way that I do. How can they? I feel like a heel so I pretend to join their celebration; I don't want to steal it from them. I know they are joyously relieved. I am not; at least not in the same way.

Many of my friends and acquaintances who have survived cancer feel this same ambivalence about the new horizon of apparent health. Is it real? we ask. Is it a horizon or an oasis? Or merely an illusion? Will it last? Is the doctor right? What about next time? Can I stop thinking about it until then? If it happens again, how will I survive? And what's this new pain I'm feeling? Is that a blemish or a mole? A tiny black and blue mark, perhaps? Was it there before? Is that a lump or just my imagination?

The most lingering malaise of a second strike is that it makes us understand just how vulnerable we are. On the first pass—at least with cancer or any serious health issue—we are made to understand that we are mortal. This is difficult enough. However, in the second round, we are made to understand that we are not only mortal, but somehow assailable; that for the finite time we have as a mortal, we are vulnerable to this disease. Or anything else for that matter. In fact, we are vulnerable to secondary illnesses that may result from the stress and/or the medications and treatments of this disease. To add insult to injury, we are told that stress will make us even more "breach-able."

I have one cancer-surviving friend who was told by her doctor to avoid "stressing her immune system." She tells me in a comic/tragic voice worthy of a Shakespearean play, "So, let's see. What he's saying is: you've had cancer. Again. Try to avoid any stress. Because stress could give it an opening to come back. Again. Is this the kind of advice that should be offered with a handful of valium, or what??"

Another friend feels almost too weary to move toward the horizon of health. She has just completed over a year of gut-wrenching, skin-burning treatments for her second bout with cancer. The cancer, they've told her, has retreated and could even be completely eradicated. No reason for her to hang back and let life pass her by. Except, of course, that she's physically depleted by the horrendous side effects of chemotherapy and radiation; and she's emotionally wrung by financial worries, employment negotiations, and decisions about treatment options including a trial program for which she may be a candidate—or may not. Also, various organs don't work too well, having been worn out by two strikes of chemo, radiation, and anti-cancer drugs. Horizon? What horizon?

It is not that we are ungrateful for right now. Most of us, myself included, thank God for healing every day. It's just that we want that new horizon to appear clearly, and we want it forever. The danger here is to become so unnerved by the new horizon that we refuse to move toward it. It can be all too easy for someone recovering from a second strike to embrace the crisis mentality, the attitude of illness. It can seem easier to maintain that diminished, low throb of pain or sorrow than to risk a run at no pain or no sorrow.

Because if we make that run and fall short, we're not sure we'll survive the disappointment or the renewed agony.

Debbie, to her distress, has seen this situation again and again. She is currently working with an elderly woman who came into the facility to recover from a fall. The woman was making slow but sure progress, participating in physical therapy, eating well, taking her medication, following all instructions faithfully. She was highly motivated and talked constantly of the day when she would return to her home of fifty years. She had only a week to go to reach that goal when she came down to a viral infection that quickly impacted her lungs and caused impaired breathing.

Debbie says that the infection was not serious as such things go, certainly not fatal. But her patient simply gave up. She fought the oxygen, pulling the tubes out of her nose. She turned her head aside to avoid the breathing machine that would help restore her lungs. She wouldn't eat anything and had to be coerced into taking broth by the threat of intravenous nutrition. The pleasant, lively woman who faced her first crisis with faith and energy collapsed into a cantankerous, shrunken shadow who rejected all efforts to encourage healing after her second strike. Even when the infection began to recede, almost in spite of its host, she refused to believe she would ever fully recover or return home.

"Basically, she gave up. Nothing we could say mattered. And what was really disturbing, but unfortunately not unusual, is that a return to good health is within her grasp. She's not that sick, and in fact, she's getting better despite herself. But she doesn't want to move forward," reports Debbie, who thinks it has a lot to do with the frightening aspect of hope. "I've seen this before. People who have been sick or downhearted for so long may get to the point where they are simply afraid to hope. I think they feel that if they muster up enough hope to move forward, and then they're disappointed again, they won't be able to stand the pain. They convince themselves it's not worth the risk. So they don't try."

Joe and Rita, whose story we read in chapter 2, understand this feeling. After five years of crisis after crisis, constant pain, and extreme frustration in seeking services and compensation, they have to fight despair even as new treatments and the end to their legal battle looms on the horizon. Joe describes the temptation he works to resist every day, "I want to go where God leads me through this, but sometimes I'm just afraid to try. And now that I have some really great opportunities—doing more catering, getting out of the house more, investigating new treatments—I really have to prepare myself mentally to move forward. I can't let my fear get in the way."

This can be a serious temptation for people in crisis who see a new horizon within their reach. Moving toward that horizon will require a real commitment and hard work; it is much easier just to stay on familiar ground, even when that ground is a bit rocky. In her book, *For Your Own Good*, psychologist Alice Miller explores how people can become trapped in an unhealthy cycle of crises. Often because they've been abused as children, as was the case with Violet, or neglected, they simply cannot imagine taking the risk of trying to reach a better place.

Miller offers an example from a television news/talk show: "A twenty-four-year-old woman who has been addicted to heroin since age sixteen appears on TV and explains that she supports her habit by means of prostitution...she makes a very sincere impression...only the matter-of-factness with which she regards this vicious circle as the only possible way of life for her puzzles us. This woman obviously cannot imagine a different life, free of her addiction."

Miller theorizes that the only way to break such a "vicious circle" is for the victim to honestly seek out and face her authentic feelings, and to become a gentle, loving witness to the child inside her.

To Violet, this sounds very much like what she is trying to do. Yet she echoes Miller in acknowledging that it is not easy for someone who is accustomed to being abused or crushed by the circumstances of life to consciously pursue a new horizon. She admits to many a day where the best she can do is stay still. But instead of rebuking herself for these times of non-movement she has learned to look at them as "resting in the Lord. When I look at the Bible, there are many places where we are urged to lay down our burdens and rest in the Lord. I think that's good advice, especially when working toward a new life. I just don't have all it takes to do it myself. I need God to get me there. I look at it this way: God has provided the new horizon; he'll provide a way to get there. There's nothing wrong with taking a rest. As long as I don't give up."

Christian writer Joni Woelfel perhaps best captures the extraordinary properties of hope and new horizons in a reflection she offered for a column on hope by Tom Roberts, editor of the *National Catholic Reporter*. In Roberts' "Inside NCR" column, Joni observes, "Hope to me is revealing itself as an image. In her book, *Reflections in the Light*, Shakti Gawain writes, 'We expect to hit bottom, but instead we fall through a trap door into a bright new world. We have discovered the world of our spirit.' Hope as that trap door is a symbol we can all relate to in our personal and collective struggles. To hit bottom through suffering, injustice, grief and travesty—and to believe that there is no way out or help is unthinkable. Hope is a spiritual instinct that insists that the trap door is there. During our darkest times, even when our best efforts and prayers seem to bring dismal results, envisioning that sacred trap door gives us something to hold on to that we can be sure of. In our heart of hearts, through commitment to faith, we know it is there."

Amen.

TALKING IT OVER WITH GOD

Lord, sometimes the hardest moment in healing comes when the end is in sight. When I had my first glimpse of that new horizon, still so far away and hard to believe in, it was at once the most exciting and frightening moment since this new crisis struck me down.

I want to get there, Lord, but I just don't know if I can. I'm excited about the prospect of new hope, new ways, a new chance, even a new life. At the same time, I'm terrified by everything that is new right now. I'm afraid to give up the ways I'm accustomed to. I'm worried that this new horizon is merely an illusion, that it won't be all it seems to be when I arrive, that I'll have made the arduous trip for nothing. I don't want to be disappointed. I wonder if I have the courage for the journey; if I can overcome everything I still must overcome to get there.

Lord, help me to banish my fear and doubt. Let the hope and excitement of a new horizon overcome my fear and uncertainty. You've taught me to take baby steps, Lord; now teach me to stride, and soon, to run!

ASK YOURSELF

1. Which horizon do you prefer: the eastern horizon where the sun rises, or the western horizon where the sun sets?

2. Can you describe a time in your life when the appearance of a new horizon has brought you both hope and fear?

3. When a new horizon materializes in your life, are you most likely to approach it cautiously or run toward it with abandon?

TAKING FURTHER ACTION

• Listen to a recording of the hymn *Amazing Grace*, or read the lyrics in a hymnal. Experience both the joy and fear of the words as they reflect God's gift of a new horizon.

• Read Noah's story in Genesis, chapters 6—9. Instead of concentrating on the familiar drama of destruction, pay attention to Noah's long wait for a new horizon and how he handled all the responsibilities that first sight brought him.

• Whether you want to admit it or not, your troubles have created a new horizon in your life. It may not be a horizon you wish to approach. It may not be the horizon you expected at this time of your life. But it is there. Play the "what if" game with your new horizon. Ask yourself three questions: What if I embrace this new horizon? What if I just stay where I am and refuse to move in any direction? What if I run in the opposite direction from this new horizon?

Play each possibility all the way through. Take the time to completely envision what you think would happen in each of the three "what if" scenarios. Remember there is no right answer for everyone; indeed, there may be no right answer for you. Don't approach this exercise with the determination to resolve on one scenario. Simply explore the three prospects. You may end up being less fearful of the horizon when you realize you have a choice as to how or whether you approach it.

CHAPTER ELEVEN

MORE LIGHTNING

*So Abraham...sent her away. When the water in the skin was gone,
she cast the child under one of the bushes...she said, "Do not let me
look on the death of the child." And as she sat opposite of him, she
lifted up her voice and wept.*   Genesis 21:14–16

From the time Abram and his wife, Sarai, bought Hagar and
attached her to their caravan, the Egyptian girl's life was one strike
after another. Her horizons looked bleak. She was taken from her
family and land to travel with what must have seemed to her crazy
nomads who worshiped an unfamiliar God. She was enslaved. She
was forced to be a concubine to Abram. She was made to bear his
son, and then immediately give the baby up to Sarai. She was hated
by her jealous mistress. She was banished with her young son to the
desert. And finally, she sat in that desert, certain she was watching
her son die. Clearly Hagar understood the concept of recurring
tragedy.

Anyone who's faced returning trouble, or a second strike, knows
that the crisis does not end immediately after the lightning hits. In
fact, that's usually only the beginning, and just about everyone
who's mustered the courage to move toward a new horizon knows

this. The sparks from that second strike can scatter and start small and large conflagrations that will flare up for some time. And surprisingly, those flaring flames are as capable of causing serious burns as any lightning bolt.

I was sitting on the examining table about five weeks after my second strike, which had been a new melanoma found after six years had passed since my first bout with this skin cancer. In those ensuing five weeks, I had undergone seven new biopsies; my doctor and I and my husband had decided that such an aggressive schedule would bring us the quickest sense of peace. The optimistic strategy was working—the first melanoma had been successfully and completely eradicated, and the new biopsies had all come back blessedly negative.

Until now. My doctor looked directly at me and I knew what was coming even before he said, "Just when we finally thought things were getting simple again...". He went on to explain that the pathologist had found the beginning of another melanoma; as he put it "sort of a half-a-melanoma." Of course, this half-a-melanoma would require a whole 'nother surgery to remove all the skin around the area. The surgery would be immediate—as in now; I would not even leave this examining table—even though the stitches had not yet been removed from the first cut. And even more devastating to my suddenly fragile self-image and vanity, this one was just above my breast; it would be the first scar that would be visible every time I wore a collarless dress or blouse.

My heart sunk. I mean, it actually sunk into my stomach. I could feel it. I hadn't even recovered from the initial second strike, over a month ago. In fact, I had nowhere near recovered from that shock; I was still reeling and trying to find my footing on the foundation of faith I'd so carefully constructed. And now this?? What was this, anyway? Part two of strike two?

How can I even describe the feeling? The closest thing I can think of was something that happened to me as a child. On the hottest of summer days, my parents would pack my sister and I into our old blue, hat-shaped Chevy and drive nearly an hour to a beach in Rhode Island. Though we had plenty of beaches in Connecticut, they were all sheltered by Long Island, and so none offered the tremendous waves that roared along Rhode Island beaches. Of course, to a child, a "tremendous" wave need be no more than a few feet high; still, summer days on the Rhode Island shore were nothing short of thrilling.

On this particular day, though, thrilling quickly became terrifying. The waves were especially high; a storm had just worked its way up the coast. Parts of the beach were roped off, so that the diligent lifeguards could stay focused on the smallest, safest areas. My parents were a bit anxious, but, loathe to ruin the day, simply told me to stay within the prescribed area. I was a strong swimmer and couldn't wait to try bodysurfing with the rest of the crowd in this swirling froth. The first few waves were exciting as I held my own admirably, surfing in to the shore and then quickly wading back out several yards to await the next wave.

Suddenly they started coming faster. The swells on the horizon were daunting. Usually at this beach there would be ten or twelve good waves and then a calm break. Not today. The waves kept coming, and to me, they seemed bigger and bigger. But I wasn't about to give in. None of the other kids in the water were wimping out and heading to their parents on the beach. I was as good a swimmer as any of them. I caught one wave just as it broke violently, and I was whirled around and slammed onto the ocean bottom. My arm and leg were scraped by stones in the sand, and by the time I managed to come to the surface, I was bruised, shaky on my feet, and scared. Then I looked up. And panicked. A second wave had been "doubling" right behind the first. I knew I wouldn't be able to ride it, nor had I caught my breath enough to dive deep under the wave and emerge on the calmer side. I hadn't even had a chance to get my feet on the ground, and all I could feel was panic.

That's how I felt when my doctor told me about "part two" of my second strike. That's how it feels: chaotic, confusing, swirling terror.

Matt's situation demonstrates even more dramatically how second strikes are not isolated incidents. He had enjoyed what he termed, "astoundingly" good health for most of his seventy-five years. He jokes now that he didn't know how lucky he was, yet he is serious when confessing how much he regrets taking his good health for granted. Within a twenty-month period it all fell apart.

It began with the death of a sister, with whom he'd been very close. Although he'd experienced people close to him dying in the past, he was especially hard hit when this particular sister died. It was a strong emotional reminder of mortality; other more physical reminders soon followed.

He began to have bone and joint pain, which, he laughs, "is not all that unusual for someone my age!" But his doctor diagnosed a bone disease and put him on Prednisone, a strong and effective drug that is also known for certain side effects. Matt wasn't thrilled about taking the medication daily, but the doctor assured him it was the best treatment for the disease. Resigned, he began the course of medication.

Within a short time a regular annual exam revealed that he had prostate cancer. Though this is well-known as a curable cancer which many men have beaten, Matt was stunned. The fact that he'd never been seriously ill in over seven decades made the news all the more difficult to absorb. He found himself unable to believe, despite all the evidence to the contrary, that he would be able to go on and live a normal life after the cancer. It was his wife of forty-nine years, Jennifer, a very practical woman who'd weathered a few of her own health storms, who helped him cope. She arranged for a consultation and went along with him to make certain they'd both fully understand his options. She called a family conference, and both their daughters came armed with information they'd researched on the Internet. Together, they decided on a course of treatment and met with the doctor again.

"Jen and the girls were terrific, amazing," declares Matt, still shaking his head in appreciation. "If it had been up to me, I'd still be sitting around wondering what to do. It wasn't so much that I was scared; I'd just never been sick before, never had to consider these things. Of course, eventually I got scared!" By then, though, he'd started to remember how much he had to be thankful for. The cancer had been found early and was therefore easier to treat. His doctors and technicians were sensitive and helpful. Matt also looked for "signs along the way" that helped remind him of God's presence. "There was a pane of stained glass in the treatment room. It was blue, and I've always thought of blue as a calming, healing color," he recalls. "So every time I walked in there, I looked at it and said to myself, 'Thank you, God.'"

While his deep faith and his family sustained him through the discomfiting treatment, Matt now acknowledges, "I might not have gotten through it all if I'd known what was coming."

The man who'd never been sick suddenly found himself in the midst of the sickest year of his life. Barely a month had passed between his last cancer treatment and the day when he noticed that his leg was bothering him. Having learned the value of early intervention, he and Jen made an appointment with a vascular specialist. After several tests, an ultrasound of his aorta revealed the presence of a "triple A," or an abdominal aortic aneurysm, lurking in the region behind his navel. Although the doctor determined that the aneurysm was "smaller than the dangerous size," he also said it would need to be watched and, if it grew, immediately removed.

"Although the doctor was not concerned about immediate danger, the news really threw both Jen and I for a loop," Matt confirms. "It was not so much that it was a dire situation, but coming on the heels of the cancer, it definitely got my attention. I'm a pretty accepting person, but I really had to use my faith to keep from letting my imagination run away with me."

Matt and Jen did their best to live as normal a life as possible, but as summer dragged on, he began to feel increasingly ill. It was not, as they might have feared, the aorta; regular check-ups indicated no change there. They were mystified, and increasingly worried. "I just felt really sick," Matt says. "In fact, I actually felt sicker with whatever this was than I had felt with the first two serious diseases. I had severe, debilitating headaches. What I didn't know was what the doctors soon discovered. At seventy-three, I had diabetes! Who could have imagined it?"

Although this disease was arguably the most treatable and least likely to be fatal of all those Matt had faced in a few short months, for the first time he sank into depression. "For some reason, this one was the hardest to take," he said, adding candidly, "for one thing, I really love to cook and eat. That means a lot to me, and it's a big part of our family life—getting together for food. So when that was severely limited, I started feeling deprived and depressed! To make matters worse, the doctors acknowledged that the Prednisone can make diabetes worse, but they don't have a better prescription for the joint and bone disease. So I was really feeling kind of stuck there for awhile."

Before Matt could get "unstuck," a routine follow-up exam showed a possible problem with his prostate—again. "It was almost a year to the date from the first cancer," Matt said, shaking his head in disbelief. However, when a biopsy came back negative, he simply proclaimed, "Thank you, God!"

It is one of his favorite sayings, and he has relied on it over the past two years. Not once, even during his brief depression after discovering the diabetes, did he consider ceasing in his praise and thanksgiving. How has he managed to sustain his faith through multiple health strikes? Describing himself as very realistic, he explains, "For one thing, I learned to just stop worrying. It sounds impossible, and it might have been, but I made a decision to do it. I refuse to sit around and dwell on all this. I'd still be depressed if I did that."

He also turned to many pragmatic spiritual and emotional aids, including Jen and his daughters, Bible readings, innumerable games of Yahtzee, and transcendental meditation, a practice he took up over thirty years ago and which he describes as "not a religion, but a practice that will make your religion stronger. I already have a very strong sense of God, and I think this is just one way I can feel closer to God. In the end, though, the most important thing to me is grace. I don't usually pray for myself—for a certain outcome or result—but I do pray for the grace to handle whatever comes my way."

Matt also attributes his positive outlook and determination to live life fully to a strong sense of discipline. As many of us have discovered, it is a vital component to first, surviving multiple strikes, and then, moving forward. One woman, a victim of childhood sexual abuse who as a result made one bad decision after another as she became an adult, describes her practice of discipline as "acting as if." For her, acting as if means to do the things you know you should do—even if they are the last things you feel like doing. It is, in essence, acting as if you are capable of moving forward and have indeed started. She explains how she implemented the technique after falling into a prolonged depression over the state of her adult life and the burden of her ruined childhood.

"One morning I was lying in bed—and that's about all I did at that time, lie in bed—thinking about how pathetic and wretched I was. I'd finally been reduced to skipping my therapy sessions, the one thing I had, at least, been making myself do. Now I'd stopped even doing that much. I didn't get up. I kept all my shades drawn in the house, so I didn't really know, or care, whether it was night or day. I didn't get dressed. I only showered when I couldn't stand myself. I'd unplugged the phone so I didn't have to listen to worried messages from the few friends I had left or frustrated calls from my therapist reminding me I'd missed yet another session. My job was so lame and useless that I didn't even bother calling in sick anymore.

"On this particular morning, I started thinking about suicide.

But strangely enough it didn't hold any appeal to me, and even more strangely, I took a bizarre sense of hope from that. Can you imagine grasping hope from the fact that you don't want to commit suicide?? So I started thinking, 'OK, what do you want to do, then?' I remembered some tests my therapist had given me that showed how capable I could be when I applied myself. At that time, he had reminded me of how many skills I'd used to survive my childhood, and even though I'd been damaged by that childhood, I had not lost the discipline I needed to live through it.

"At the time he told me that, I just thought to myself, 'Yeah, yeah, right.' But now I actually tried to remember how I did it as a kid, how I survived. What I would do as a little girl was to pretend, to act, like it wasn't me all this stuff was happening to. I pretended that it was another little girl living through all this; meanwhile, I would act as if I was a different kid. A kid who went to school, which I made myself do even when my father said school was a stupid waste of time. A kid who washed up every day, even though no one cared whether I was clean or not. A kid who read, even though I had to beg books from my teachers and classmates. All those things, according to my therapist, helped me develop the skills I needed to survive.

"So laying in bed that morning, I wondered if I could use them now. I figured, 'Well, if you really don't want to die, you might as well try to live again.' And I started acting as if. I acted as if therapy could really help, so I went. I acted as if I might feel better about myself if I showered and dressed every day, so I did. I acted as if I had a reason to get out of the bed in the morning, so I made myself get up every day and make the bed. I acted as if getting any job might lead to a better one, so I started to apply for openings.

"I guess you could say this worked. I'm not saying I felt good doing it. I didn't! I resented acting as if. It was hard. Doing things because you know you should, when every fiber of your being doesn't want to, can be horribly difficult. I wanted to quit every single morning. But I didn't, and after awhile there were a few things I actually started enjoying. I began to look forward to dressing every day, and was amazed when a check-out clerk said I had 'a flair' for clothes. I was surprised about how much I liked the light in the morning when I made myself pull up the shades and let it in. In fact I started going to bed with all the shades up so I could have the first light!

"I'm liking more about my life all the time. But I still don't like the alarm clock!"

Who does? But when God sends us a wake-up call, we may all need to act as if.

TALKING IT OVER WITH GOD

O Lord, here we go again! How can I help but feel betrayed? I thought I was making progress! I thought the end of this nightmare was in sight. I thought you were working with me, Lord! Was I wrong? I don't understand this backsliding, these new flashes of lightning that must be quenched before they start an raging blaze. I don't know if I have the energy to take up this new battle when I thought the war was just about over.

But wait. I will not give ways to doubt and fear. I've come too far. You've given me a strong foundation in faith, and I will not abandon it now. This is the time for me to draw on what you've given me. This is not the only obstacle, the only adversity I will face in my life. I have to face that fact. I may not know what to do right now; I may be weary and sad and disappointed. I am all those things. Yet, I know you are right here, beside me, Lord. You were working with me, Lord, and you are still working me. And if I've learned anything, I've learned this: you will always work with me, Lord! And now, exhausted and battle-weary, I will do the one thing I can do: wait upon the Lord.

Ask Yourself

1. What do you find more difficult when dealing with a crisis: its onset, or the many new troubles that accompany it?
2. Have you ever believed there was "light at the end of the tunnel," only to have darkness suddenly fall again?
3. Do you think there's value to "acting as if"?

Taking Further Action

• Read Pat Conroy's novel *Beach Music*. Pay attention to how the various characters separately address the continuing sorrows and repeated tragedies in their lives to either seek or avoid healing— both in themselves and others.

• Read Hagar's story in Genesis, chapters 16 and 21, to get a full understanding of her sorrows, strength, and ultimate faith.

• Go to a quiet, darkened place: your room, a church, a library cubicle, any place that is silent and dim. Close your eyes and imagine yourself in a tunnel suddenly plunged into darkness as you were at the onset of your current situation. Stay calm. Remember how you dealt with those initial moments and days. See how the light slowly filtered in as you began to cope through the beginning of this crisis. Recall what you did, how you prayed, who you turned to; and savor your slow success in coping. These form the shape and structure of the tunnel, as well as the path to the light at the end of it.

When you are ready, when you have recalled and memorized every positive detail thus far in the crisis, let the tunnel again become dark. Don't panic. Understand that each crisis brings its times of light and dark; realize that this new darkness is only temporary and that it will pass. You have not retreated from the progress you've made. The same faith and skills that served you thus far remain present in and around you.

Now that it is dark again, take a moment to rest. When you are ready, begin to reassert that faith and those skills that have brought you so far along. Know that eventually, the glimmering periods of light will become longer and the darkness will abate until you are once again in the light.

CHAPTER TWELVE

SURRENDER

She had endured much under many physicians, and had spent all that she had; and she was not better, but rather grew worse. She had heard about Jesus, and came up behind him in the crowd and touched his cloak, for she said, "If I but touch his clothes, I will be made well."   Mark 5:25–28

For the woman with a hemorrhage, Jesus is quite literally a last resort. Everyone else had failed her. Everything else had failed her. For us, taught to turn to Jesus as a first resort, this doesn't sound quite right, but remember that this woman didn't know Jesus was God; she had only heard rumors about his healing power. He was all she had left. In this she is very much like all who have experienced recurring crises, particularly those of us who have been felled by strikes within strikes as discussed in the previous chapter. Imagine the act of surrender it took for her to reach out and touch his ragged, dusty cloak.

The last thing anyone fighting for his or her life can imagine doing is to surrender. After all, surrender is the opposite of victory; surrender means giving up and giving in. Surrender is for cowards, right?

Not if the surrender means turning to God. Those of us who

have experienced multiple strikes must redefine our notion of surrender. Surrender doesn't mean giving in to an illness or addiction or despair. It doesn't mean giving in to the worst part of ourselves. It doesn't mean giving in to the temptation to give up. In fact, in our circumstances, surrender in the context of faith is not a negative action; it doesn't mean giving up at all.

In his book *Spiritual Surrender: Yielding Yourself to a Loving God*, James A. Krisher suggests that surrender is more an act of heroism than cowardice. Acknowledging that the word surrender "implies being a loser...servility, submissiveness, and obedience to established authorities...a kind of passive resignation that simply accepts everything as it is," Krisher contends: "In fact, for the Christian, living the surrendered life often means not quitting, but actively persisting in worldly struggles even when we may want to stop. Living the surrendered life often means not accepting things as they are, but working with God to change them."

Surrender means giving ourselves to God; with all our flaws, all our sorrows, all our diseases, all our failures, with all the strikes against us. Surrender is a conscious decision to acknowledge God's loving power and a conscious effort to give ourselves over to that power. It is an admission on our part that, finally, God is in charge, and that we will trust the outcome of God's plan. Krisher explains, "Thus spiritual surrender is not like the crushing experience of surrender to an enemy, which leaves us broken and shame-filled. Our God is not a general who uses brute force to coerce our submission and who delights in breaking our will. No, spiritual surrender is a deliberate act of the will, not a breaking of the will."

It is also not easy! Many of us have to come to within a breath of despair or even death before we can bring ourselves to surrender to God. In this we are not so different from the woman with the hemorrhage who touches the edge of Christ's robe. Perhaps we should know better—after all, as we've observed, she didn't know who Jesus really was and we do—but human nature is stubborn. We want to have control, and we cling to the illusion of that control, for that is all it is, for as long as we can. Only those who have experienced multiple strikes can truly understand how courageous that poor, sick woman really was.

Another extraordinarily courageous woman touched my life not long ago. A fellow contributor to *Daily Guideposts,* Mary Jane Clark experienced one of the most harrowing first strikes a person could have: the loss of a spouse. Widowed with several children, she used her faith and an abiding strength to soldier on. She eventually remarried a wonderful man and built a joyful life with him, only to learn that she had cancer. This second strike barely slowed her down. Far from surrendering in the negative sense of giving in, Mary Jane girded herself for a long fight. With the unwavering support of her husband and their children, she sought out and researched the best possible treatment centers and programs. Between treatments, she and her husband continued to travel, visiting their children all over the world.

For a while the cancer seemed to be in remission. But it lurked, waiting, and eventually came back. Too soon, the fires from that second strike flared. Mary Jane continued to fight, all the while surrendering to God in a way that embodied the concept of grace. She kept her far-flung friends and colleagues apprised of her status through beautiful and often quite funny e-mails. It was in one of these e-mails that she informed us, after months and months of drugs and radiation and specialists, that she was throwing a party to celebrate her life because she'd decided to cease all treatment. She assured us that she wasn't ruling out a miracle; indeed she hoped for one. However, while she waited, she was completing the surrender to God that had characterized her entire life.

The final e-mail from her address came from her husband not long after the party to let us know that the most wonderful woman he'd ever known had gone home to God.

Perhaps surrender was hard for Mary Jane, but she certainly

made it look simple. It may be all but impossible to imagine how she did it—or to imagine doing it ourselves. Yet it must be observed that Mary Jane never surrendered to death. She surrendered to God. Long before the cancer, she learned to live the surrendered life. It is that, and not the way she handled her last days and death, that makes her unusual: many of us must be forced by bruising circumstances to even consider this kind of surrender.

Yet there comes a point in the life of every person who has been bowed by recurring tragedy where surrender to God becomes a clear option. Some reject it. Some struggle against it. Many struggle with it. It is true that most of us do not possess Mary Jane's grace, and so the struggle can be monumental. We may not be able to imagine God loving us enough for us to trust in surrender. We may be the worse kind of control freaks. We may think we're fixing the situation all by ourselves. We may be simply afraid. And sometimes it does indeed take reaching the point of weary desperation before we can give ourselves up to God. Everyone who has spoken in these pages describes somehow coming to face the option of surrender.

Marion Bond West describes scraping the bottom of the desperation barrel before traveling through the tunnel to the light of surrender in *The Nevertheless Principle*. In a passage many of us can identify with, she describes how she had to be almost forced to the point of surrendering to God: "I told God, 'I can't live without him (her husband who was dying of cancer). You need to understand that.' I ran as though hot lava were on my heels. 'Don't let go! Hold on!' something inside me kept screaming. It never occurred to me that victory might lie in exactly the opposite direction. But letting go never once entered my mind."

Yet Marion did learn to let go; in fact, she later describes how joy eventually came flooding back into her life when God gave her certain images that allowed her to totally trust him. And yes, total trust is exactly what is required for total surrender. But those of us who have not yet reached Mary Jane's state of grace or Marion's utter surrender to the "God of Nevertheless" should not be disheartened. Surrender can be as much a journey as a juncture; even then, it is no easy trip. Many of us will travel the road a long, long time before reaching that place where we empty ourselves before God. We need to remember that every small step forward is, in itself, a kind of blessed surrender. Therefore, we must remember to take the time to celebrate each of those steps as though they were magnificent strides—for they truly are.

. It was a long time before Kathryn, the Maine woman who lost her son and her husband within a few short months, could even imagine celebrating. Her surrender was more a journey of faith than a revelation, and her steps were accompanied by the sound of her granddaughter's laughter, the only laughter the family heard on that first Christmas; the excited whispers at the wedding shower she attended almost two years later for her daughter; the shouts of joy at the graduation of her son on one sunny May afternoon; the happy cries of neighborhood children at play near her new home in Savannah.

"It took awhile before I could really face God and understand that I was still loved, that I'd always been loved. I'd been loved even through all that, probably especially through all that, if only I'd realized it at the time," she says softly, more than a decade after that year of tragedies. She wastes no time chastising herself for the pace of her journey. "And I can finally say (of her husband and son) that God gave them to me, and then took them away. They were his to give and his to have now. And I know now we will all be his to reunite someday."

Joe and Rita are both conscious of the possibility for surrender, and though they are sister and brother, they know they are in different places on the path. Joe, perhaps because of his acute pain, has been driven farther along the path of surrender, deliberately opening himself to follow God's lead in matters like serving at morning Mass and forcing himself to accept catering jobs. Rita, on the other hand, is still angry and frustrated, and she knows this prevents her from moving toward surrender as rapidly as she may wish. Her obstacles are easily understood; as Joe's caretaker, she is acutely aware of precisely what happened to him and how deeply they have both suffered. Joe did not make the choice to have his entire life disrupted and changed forever, while Rita, as his caretaker, *did* make that choice; surrender for her, therefore, may be harder to achieve.

"I just don't understand why—how—all this has happened to him," says Rita, shaking her head. "And I can't understand how, all these years later, we still have no real resolutions." Still, she understands her own emotions and is taking positive steps to build up her own spirituality. In addition to participating in the support group and her church, she is taking the initiative to spend more time doing things she enjoys—without Joe. She has signed up for a yoga class, plans shopping evenings with co-workers, and intends to learn Italian for a trip to Italy she is planning.

Joe is enthusiastically cheering her on. "One of the worst things about what happened to me is what it did to Rita," he declares. "She has given up everything for me. She was there in the emergency room that first night after the accident, and she's been by my side, fighting for me, ever since. Neither of us expected our lives to turn out this way, and I completely understand her anger. Sometimes I think she carries the burden of her anger *and* my anger! It's no wonder. She has seen me at my absolute worst. The fact that we still love each other is a miracle. Literally! So, I couldn't be happier to see her trying to do some things for herself."

For Cary, the woman who suffers from recurring Lyme Disease, the path to surrender has been more of an internal trek. Much like the hemorrhaging woman who sought Jesus, she's found little in the way of help or healing from those "experts" she's turned to in the outside world. So she has learned to concentrate on her inner spirituality, developing her faith through constant prayer. Indeed, she's found ways to use her illness to promote this effort, often allowing weariness to lead her to God. "Sometimes I'm just so exhausted with everything, all the efforts to find help and under-standing," she explains. "At those times, I simply turn to God and say, 'You will have to handle this. I can't. I don't have the answers, and I won't have them until you give them to me.'"

Jeffrey and Susan have not so much sought surrender as they have let the obstacles in their lives lead them to surrender. At first there was no way they could perceive losing both their jobs within a few months as a possible spiritual experience. They certainly did not see it as a gift. But they eventually learned to acknowledge the power of surrender as they began to recover from their employ-ment disasters. "I think we only realized how vital surrender was to the process after we'd done it," says Susan. "It was only once we'd accepted what had happened—including the rejection of those around us—and had become more involved in our church, that we began to see God's hand in all this.

"It took a while for us to understand that the one thing we need-ed to do was admit that God had a better plan for us. That's when we could see the positive aspects of everything that had seemed so negative. God's plan had allowed us to see who our friends really were. God's plan had brought us back to a good church. God's plan had forced us to recognize what was really important in our lives. God's plan was very likely to bring us new and different work prospects. At that point, how could we doubt the value of giving ourselves to God's plan?"

Betty has come to understand that her whole life, with its many losses and disappointments has been one long invitation from God to embrace his gift of grace. Hindsight has allowed her to compre-hend how God has used her active surrender to help others in trou-ble. Looking back on what was a painful string of life losses, she observes that once she surrendered, she came to understand "how God used the good and the bad events of my life to mold me into someone who could be used by him. I can look back today and...I am most thankful for the times that were the most difficult, for those times of suffering brought about the most changes in me and, at the same time, gave me a greater understanding of how God wants us to take what we've gained in his classroom of life and share it with others."

For Robert and other addicts, surrendering to God is simply part and parcel of their sobriety. The tenets of Alcoholics Anonymous and associated Twelve-step programs require the individual to literally "give up" to God or, as they say, the "Higher Power." As Robert explains, "It is not only about giving up the addiction. In fact, it's really about understanding that we don't even have the power to give up the addiction! The only power we have is to admit that we have no power. And that God—that's why we say 'Higher Power'— has all of it. So it's a complete surrender to God, an absolute acknowledgment that we are helpless in and of ourselves."

People who have suffered repeated abuse, like Violet, often have the hardest time accepting surrender as a form of spiritual victory. Though they rationally know that surrender to God is different from surrendering to another person, they have spent their lives suffering because they've abrogated their will to another. For the abused person, surrender is usually something to be "unlearned" rather than grasped at. Violet admits that she is still working on the concept, and that she has to keep reminding herself that surrendering to God is completely different from the self-destructive "giving in" she has done in the past.

"I feel like I have to balance two things here. One is that I don't ever need to give up what I want or compromise what I feel is right for myself because of what someone else demands from me. That's something I'm continuing to work on in therapy, and it is a key to my healing and taking control of my life. At the same time, though, I know that I need—no, that I want—to follow the direction God lays out for me. And that involves giving in to God," Violet says. She concludes, "Believe me, it's quite a balancing act, and I'm not sure I've figured it out yet."

In *Spiritual Surrender*, author Krisher empathizes with the many of us who haven't quite "figured it out yet." Knowing that surrender is anything but a quick fix, he writes, "Spiritual surrender should not be viewed, then, as providing a pious escape from the reality of suffering. It does not mean that we will be spared what others must endure, or be able to glide through the worst in a cloud of tranquillity. It did not mean this for Jesus, who was utterly yielded to his Father, and it will not mean this for us."

Regardless of where we are in our journey, we must not consider ourselves failures if we have not achieved complete surrender. After all, what is needed to reach such an extraordinary objective is nothing less than what Jesus offered God at that most terrifying moment in the Garden of Gethsemane: utter capitulation to the will of the Father, no matter how agonizing the suffering that would result from that surrender. None of us are Jesus. We may not even be capable of such absolute surrender. Yet we can take comfort in and even celebrate our efforts. All we need do is keep the goal in sight, and never stop trying.

TALKING IT OVER WITH GOD

Lord, it's difficult to think of surrender as a good thing. I've been taught to think that only a coward surrenders; or just as bad, only those who know they can't possibly win. It goes against everything I've learned and believe to give in. Help me to remember, Lord, that I when I surrender to you, I am not giving in to disease, addiction, abuse, self-denigration, or harmful behaviors. Indeed, by surrendering to you, I am acknowledging that you, and you alone, can lead me to victory over the troubles in my life.

Obviously, as evidenced by this recurring crisis, I'm not succeeding on my own. I can't, because after all, I am your creation: I need my Creator and Parent to lift me up, to show me when to go to battle and when to retreat.

Lord, you yourself surrendered to the divine will by allowing yourself to be crucified. In so doing, you saved the world and redeemed us all—including me! Remind me of this when I struggle to yield myself to you. Teach me again and again the joy of such surrender, for it is the rejoicing of Easter. And, Lord, I desperately need this joyful surrender now.

ASK YOURSELF

1. Do you think you've ever truly experienced the joy of surrendering to God?

2. What aspects of yielding your life to God are most enticing and exciting?

3. What aspects of utter surrender to God are most frightening?

TAKING FURTHER ACTION

• Read James A. Krisher's book, *Spiritual Surrender: Yielding Yourself to a Loving God.*

• In Mark 5:25–34, read the story of the surrender and subsequent healing of the hemorrhaging woman who turned to Jesus.

• If the idea of completely surrendering every aspect of your crisis and your life to God is overwhelming, think small! Identify a smaller part or problem in your life that you would really love to surrender to God—something you just can't wait to get rid of! Practice the art of surrender with this one portion of your life.

On one side of a sheet of paper, write down all the emotions you think you would feel if you did surrender this issue to God. Read them over and allow yourself to feel the stirrings of each emotion: relief, joy, etc. On the other side of the paper, write down three actions you can take towards surrendering this part of your life to God. Know that these may not be easy, especially if you are a "control" person. Arrange them in order like a plan. Execute it, always keeping in mind the wonderful feelings awaiting you when you've successfully surrendered this to God.

CHAPTER THIRTEEN

TRANSFORMATIONS

Bartimaeus, son of Timaeus, a blind beggar, was sitting by the roadside. When he heard that it was Jesus of Nazareth, he began to shout out and say, "Jesus, Son of David, have mercy on me!" Many sternly ordered him to be quiet, but he cried out even more loudly, "Son of David, have mercy on me!" Then Jesus said to him, "What do you want me to do for you?" The blind man said to him, "My teacher, let me see again." Jesus said to him, "Go; your faith has made you well." Immediately he regained his sight and followed him on the way.　　　　　　　　　　　　　Mark 10:46–52

On this particular day, the blind man did not expect to be healed of his blindness at all. Indeed, the only "healing" he sought, was the temporary healing of his poverty. Bartimaeus was begging, all right, but not for his sight. He needed money. In fact, sight may have been the farthest thing from his mind; readers are given the vague impression that he was fairly comfortable in his lifestyle.

Though he was blind, Bartimaeus had been apparently blind from birth and had evidently adapted well. He was a well-known beggar, a familiar sight to passersby and his neighbors. He probably considered the excited crowd drawn by Jesus' visit a terrific opportunity to raise more cash than usual. Some biblical scholars have even suggested that, at first, Bartimaeus fully intended to ask Jesus for money. Yet when Jesus beckoned and Bartimaeus finally stood before him, the beggar abandoned his usual cry for mercy—which may well have been his daily begging cry—and asked for sight.

So what happened when Jesus healed his eyes rather than his wallet? Transformation.

However, when we manage to absorb and then fully comprehend the type and extent of healing we've received, the result can only be complete transformation.

Not only does Bartimaeus blurt out a plea for sight instead of money at the last moment, everything in and about him is transformed when he receives that sight. Without thinking he willingly leaves his "workplace"—the corner where he's spent his life begging—and immediately follows Jesus. It may be presumed that he follows Jesus away from his corner, away from his neighborhood, away even from his home and family.

Now, remember that Bartimaeus was not the average guy who, upon hearing or seeing Jesus, was so intrigued he decided to follow. No. Bartimaeus was likely to not have strayed from within a few yards of his home and his corner ever before in his life! Restricted by his disability and the need to stay near people who were familiar with him, Bartimaeus had probably never left his village. He did not possess even the limited sophistication or experience of Jesus' other disciples. And yet, without hesitation, without a worry for his sustenance or future, he jumped up to follow wherever Jesus will lead.

For all of us as well, transformation is nothing less than recognizing God and finally comprehending that God is with us and within us. While we may claim to know this through faith teachings, transformation doesn't really occur until we feel it through our own witness. As those of us who have progressed through recurring sorrows know, this kind of transformation is won at a price; often along the way, we may not believe it's worth it. Only afterwards can we understand the everlasting value of transformation.

Perhaps the event that most illustrates this is what many Christians may know as the "original" transformation: the transfiguration of Jesus on the mountain with Elijah and Moses. Once at the summit of the mountain, having taken Peter, James, and John along, Jesus changes even as they watch. His eyes, red-rimmed and crusted with the sand and dust of rough travel, become brilliant like the sun; his clothes, filthy and stained with much wear and the dirt of many rutted paths, become dazzling white; and then suddenly, before they can begin to absorb what they've already seen, Moses and Elijah appear before their stunned eyes, materializing at the side of the Lord and then proceeding to converse with him!

How do the three apostles know they are seeing Moses and Elijah? Does Jesus, still shimmering and awesome in their eyes, stop to introduce them? Not likely. No, they know this is Moses and this is Elijah because—they just know! They have passed into a different realm where knowledge comes from the inside out—not the other way around.

While they are still paralyzed with amazement and probably no little fear at this point, before they can even catch their collective breath, a brilliant cloud envelopes them. All but blinded as completely as Bartimaeus, they hear the Father's omniscient voice: "This is my Son, the Beloved; with him I am well pleased; listen to him!" (Matthew 17:5).

Finally, they fall to the ground in abject terror. Why? Is it because Jesus has been transfigured before their eyes? Is it because of Moses and Elijah casually talking with their master? Is it because of the relentless shining cloud? Doubtless, all these contribute to their confusion, but what flattens them, cowering, to the grass is the sound of God, the Father, Yahweh, I Am Who Am—and He is speaking to them!

God is not informing Moses and Elijah that Jesus is the Beloved

Son. He doesn't need to. They know. God's not telling those two revered prophets, whom he's just sent to visit with his son on the mountain, to listen to Jesus. They already do. God is directly communicating with Peter, James, and John. He is personally instructing them. Indeed, God is affirming what they've hoped, what they've tentatively believed, what they've wanted to know for sure.

Now they do. Because, make no mistake about it, though Jesus is transfigured on that mountain, it is Peter, James, and John who are transformed. What they thought they knew in their minds now resonates through their hearts, bodies, and souls. The dazzling clothes, the shining eyes, the prophets, the voice of the Father, all these have stripped away the bleariness in their sight, allowing them to recognize the Lord. Compelling them to recognize the Lord. And in that recognition, they experience transformation. No longer are they the hopeful but sometimes uncertain disciples. Now they are the ones who carry the vision, the presence of Christ, within their very beings.

It is important to remember that no matter how transforming the moment, transformation is seldom sudden. Peter, James, and John had already given up everything, and suffered much, to follow Jesus. Bartimaeus had been blind and begging all his life. While that one stunning, exhilarating instant may complete transformation, the process is long and sometimes arduous. Transformation does not come before surrender. Surrender does not come before those first few faltering steps toward a new horizon. Those first few faltering steps do not come before acceptance. Acceptance seldom comes before or without anguish.

So while transformation brings unspeakable joy, the process leading to transformation can be anything but joyful. Just as the very appearance of a new horizon can be unnerving, the idea of surrender-leading-to-transformation can be fearsome. This is particularly true when the "transformee" is someone who has been, like many of us, weakened and pummeled by repeated strikes.

In Sue Monk Kidd's bestselling novel, *The Secret Life of Bees*, the main character, Lily Melissa Owens, is just such a person. By the tender age of fourteen, Lily has already been abandoned as a toddler by her mother; the unwitting catalyst of a horrible accident; the victim of brutish emotional and physical abuse by her father; and the first-hand witness of horrible violence against her best friend. When we meet her, she is in desperate need of transformation, but unable to trust enough to embrace even the prospect of surrender. Lily has learned to lie pathologically, closely protect her thoughts, and live in a dream world that is infinitely better than the one she's known.

For example, when Lily herself has committed a crime and is on the run, she starts to remember reading Thoreau's *Walden Pond*, "and afterward I'd had fantasies of going to a private garden where (her father) would never find me. I started appreciating Mother Nature...in my mind she looked like Eleanor Roosevelt. I thought about her the next morning when I woke beside the creek in a bed of kudzu vines. A barge of mist floated along the water, and dragonflies, iridescent blue ones, darted back and forth like they were stitching up the air. It was such a pretty sight for a second I forgot the heavy feeling I'd carried...instead I was at Walden Pond."

Yet even when the opportunity for transformation stands before her, when she has the chance to trade her fantasies for a life that offers the potential for real joy, she finds it nearly impossible to lay down the vital defenses that have served her so well in her bruised life. This is a sadly familiar state for those of us who have experienced repeated sorrow and abuse; we can't imagine letting go of the armor that has allowed us to survive, even when the possibility of a new life—without the need for that armor—stares us in the face.

Lily first observes the incapacity of all wounded creatures to embrace freedom and a new life after she's trapped some bees in a jar. Like the rest of us who feel imprisoned, the bees soon grow lethargic, unable to fight the cruel circumstances that have brought them to such a diminished pass. After a while, convinced that it is wrong to keep the creatures, Lily unscrews the lid and bids them to fly away. She is distressed to observe that "the bees remained there, like planes on a runway not knowing they'd been cleared for take-off. They crawled on their stalk legs around the curved perimeters of the glass as if the world had shrunk to that jar. I tapped the glass, even laid the jar on its side, but those crazy bees stayed put."

For Lily, it is only through the unconditional love and protection of a series of human and spiritual mothers that she is finally able to surrender and step into the glimmering circle of transformation. Even then, she treads slowly and carefully. She needs incontrovertible, even mystical, proof of that love and protection before she can bring herself to shed the aura of tragedy that has become part and parcel of her very being. After months of tentatively gathering the evidence she needs, complete transformation comes to her in one extraordinary flash when she "turned and looked at August and Rosaleen and the Daughters (the women who'd nurtured her) on the porch. This is the moment I remember clearest of all—how I stood in the driveway looking back at them. I remember the sight of them standing there waiting. All these women, all this love, waiting."

Wait! we might want to cry, what if that moment is not so clear? What if we don't have enough evidence to risk embracing God's gift of transformation? What if our surrender has been tentative, with the shadow of an uncertain future still oppressing us? What if we're still lingering in the process and unable (unwilling?) to grasp the moment? After all, even Peter, James, and John, who lived with Jesus, still required his transfiguration to complete their transformation.

There's good news and bad news at this juncture. The good news is that for the surrendered sufferer, transformation must be a conscious decision. The bad news is that for the surrendered suffered, transformation must be a conscious decision.

Yes, it's true that God gave Peter, James, and John, not to mention

Bartimaeus and Lily, terrific transformation moments. It is also true that every person who has progressed along the path of suffering to the point of surrender is given opportunities for transformation. We may not witness a transfigured Jesus conversing with Elijah, Moses, and his Father, but our loving God makes miracles and moments available to us all the time.

The suffering soul that finally yields to God may find the moment of completed transformation in ordinary miracles like a sunset or moonrise, a blinding snowstorm or a perfect summer day, the first crocus of spring or the flaming oak of autumn, the Southwest's silent desert or Nova Scotia's raging waters. For others, the transforming instant may come in more extraordinary miracles like the healing of an illness, the safe touchdown of a disabled airplane, the escape from a raging fire, the home left intact after a tornado. The transforming event is not as important as the decision to embrace it.

As with some of the most memorable characters in literature, Sue Monk Kidd's Lily Melissa Owens offers us great hope for the power of transformation. Once she has taken the courageous, joyful decision to accept the gift of transformation, she reflects, "I believe in the goodness of imagination. A person shouldn't look too far down her nose at absurdities. Look at me. I dived into one absurd thing after another, and here I am...I wake up to wonder every day."

Loving us, God will wait for forever. We shouldn't.

Talking It Over with God

Lord, for so long I've yearned to be transformed. Or so I thought. Now that I feel on the brink, I'm uncertain and confused. Actually, I'm just plain petrified some of the time. I'm not so sure if I can handle it. I had all these expectations of what transformation would be: how it would happen, what it would feel like, what my life would be like when it was over. Now I realize that you're the Transformer and I'm only the transformee! Which means, I've come to understand, that embracing transformation means embracing your plan for me—and that may not necessarily be my plan for myself.

I admit it, Lord, I want to see the end result before I take the plunge. I now know I can't. Transformation is a matter of trust, the ultimate trust that no matter what my state is, no matter how much I change, you do not change. You are constant. You are in and through and around everyone and everything. You do not waver in your love or your presence. You have been with me in my past states, you are with me in my current state, and you will be with me in my transformed state. Help me to remember that by accepting your gift of transformation, I will make a choice to be with you.

Ask Yourself

1. What is most frightening about transformation: giving up the past or embracing the future?

2. Do you believe a person can be truly transformed, can wholly change?

3. Could it happen to you?

TAKING FURTHER ACTION

• Watch the movie *The Robe*. Note both the pain and fear Richard Burton's character finds himself almost compelled to experience after Jesus becomes the catalyst for the soldier's transformation.

• In Mark 10:46–52, read about the encounter between Jesus and Bartimaeus.

• Think back through your life until you can remember a moment of transformation. It may have been something massive and perhaps painful like the conscious realization that your parents' marriage was loveless; or it may have been something relatively small and exciting like discovering as a child that you really excelled at something like a sport, writing, or math.

Don't experience this memory as an adult who has successfully distanced yourself from the moment. Remember what it was like at that moment. Allow yourself to feel how strong an impact the experience had. Recall your emotions whether they were terror and anxiety, or joy and excitement (or, more likely, any combination of those!). Try to remember how the moment changed your life. How did it impact your decisions? Your self-confidence? Your faith? Now bring yourself back to this day, this experience, and understand that now you have a choice: you can choose transformation—if you dare!

CHAPTER FOURTEEN

GOD'S
WORK-IN-PROGRESS

Peter said to him, "I will lay down my life you." Jesus answered, "Very truly I tell you, before the cock crows, you will have denied me three times." John 13:37–38

Jesus said to Simon Peter, "Simon son of John, do you love me more than these?" He said to him, "Yes, Lord, you know that I love you." Jesus said to him...a second time, "Simon son of John, do you love me?" He said to him, "Yes, Lord; you know that I love you." Jesus said to him...a third time, "Simon son of John, do you love me?" Peter felt hurt because he said to him the third time, "Do you love me?" And he said to him, "Lord, you know everything; you know that I love you." John 21:15–17

If Peter hadn't been around during Jesus's day, God would have had to invent him! The wonderful, blustering apostle who spends as much time "putting his foot in it," as he does striving for the heavens, is about the most heartening model any of us could ever ask for. Peter could not be more flawed; nor could he be more determined to stay close to Jesus, even when that means denying his own habits, actions, and beliefs again and again and again. Peter is, quite literally, God's work-in-progress, and as such, gives the rest of us hope.

Keep in mind, and this may be the most important lesson Peter teaches us, that Peter continues to make these blunders even after he is transformed! Peter has already been up on the mountain. He has already seen Jesus, transfigured in all his glorious majesty. He has already come to recognize Jesus in his mind, heart, and body. And even within himself, Peter has seen and felt how Jesus is present, revealed, and active. Yet he still can't get it right all the time! Transformation, then, is not the end of the story. It is only the beginning. The road ahead may be as rough and uncertain as the one behind because, even once we are transformed, we are still God's works-in-progress.

Transformation does not protect us from disaster or shelter us from the new storms life will blow into our way. It does not make us immune to failure, illness, or relapse. What it does do is give us the solace and joy of knowing and feeling that God is with us throughout everything, regardless of what may happen in our lives; as Marion Bond West would say, "Never-the-less means always-the-more." We are now conscious of God being with us always-the-more.

Transformation also does not release us from our responsibility to work in concert with the Creator. Just as God was continually working in, through, and on Peter, so does the Creator seek to work in, through, and on us. Transformation allows us—as it did Peter—to recognize and welcome this work. It allows us to accept that there is still progress to made, and that God is leading the way. Too often, recovering victims of multiple strikes at first believe that experiencing transformation means an end to all of life's troubles. As Betty discovered after confronting her many losses in the real presence of God's forgiving love, troubles will always plague us, but transformation offers a different perspective on how to meet these challenges.

"Even after I'd come to recognize God's power in my life, things still went wrong," Betty says matter-of-factly. "I was laid off three times. I got heavily in debt—which I'm still struggling with, by the way! And I continued to doubt myself in terms of my work direction. I've never really been sure I'm doing what I'm supposed to do. What was different, however, was my strong feeling that God was always there with me, through it all. Incredible things—miracles, really—would happen to show me his presence just at a time when my need was greatest.

"I think the most wonderful and amazing moment was when I went to a hotel and conference center on a Saturday morning to take the test to become a librarian. As I was leaving after the test, I walked out a different way and went right by the bridal suite. I froze! I realized that this was the hotel I'd been married in so many years ago! They had completely redone the place so I hadn't recognized it at first. I stood there and this incredible feeling came over me. God had brought me full circle. I was starting a new life. It's not that it wasn't hard. It was! But, you know, God doesn't promise it's going to be easy. He just promises to be there."

Peter embodied this transforming statement from the moment Jesus ascended into heaven, leaving him utterly changed. Jesus had taken Peter through his paces, right down to cleverly forcing him to recant his triple denial. Even then, the lesson wasn't over for Peter, who couldn't keep himself from asking Jesus what was to become of another disciple, John. It is easy to sense that Peter expresses a touch of jealousy in this question; John is known as the "disciple whom Jesus loved."

So even after Jesus had given him power over the new church, Peter still isn't completely satisfied. And so Jesus, probably suppressing a grin and heaving an inward sigh, answers, "If it is my will that he (John) remain until I come, what is that to you? Follow me!" Thus Jesus's last words to Peter—Peter the rock, Peter the chosen one, Peter who has been forgiven all—must still be a gentle chastisement and a not so gentle reminder.

Peter would certainly need both, because at that moment when Jesus physically disappeared, Peter's worldly troubles were just beginning. What he'd suffered as a disciple of the man Jesus would prove to be nothing compared to what he was about to suffer as the leader of the Lord God's new church.

Peter would be persecuted, beaten and, despite being an unsophisticated fishermen, forced to make weighty, complex political and religious decisions. He would frequently find himself toe-to-toe with purists like his friend, James, and brilliant, well-educated orators like the stranger, Paul.

Yet Peter, knowing the responsibility to shape the church was his, dug down and managed to prevail. Not because, as had been the case in the past, he stubbornly insisted on his own way, his own instincts. No. For the first time in his life, he was ready to be shaped in every way, in every decision by God. When Peter was determined to insist that all new converts maintain strict Hebrew rules, including circumcision, God instructed him to announce a break with centuries of Jewish law. Can anyone imagine the old Peter agreeing to shelf the sacred traditions that had defined his entire life? Yet without hesitation, he decreed a new order.

Finally, after a second lifetime of bowing to God's will, he would choose to be crucified upside down so as not to suffer any less than Jesus had. Yet Peter, the man who had counseled Jesus not to speak of that nasty first crucifixion, never faltered in embracing these agonies. His Lord was with him.

And it is here that those of us who have suffered our own agonies can fearlessly address the question: why does God allow the suffering of those who love him? After all, few—including us—have suffered as deeply and for as long as the early disciples, those who loved God enough to give their lives for him. It is the age-old question that cannot be avoided. Nor perhaps can it be answered, at least not in a way that satisfies our limited human minds.

Many answers have been advanced. In *Spiritual Surrender*, James Krisher identifies a number of them. Some posit that God wants the victim of suffering to learn something from the experience, to change behavior as a result. Or they suggest that God sends a crisis to force a specific change in the victim's life. For example, a man who suffers a heart attack may come to believe that God wants him to spend more time with family.

Yet Krisher wisely dismisses these so-called reasons: "Each of these explanations presumes that suffering is God's doing, and so we have to find a way to justify God for doing it. But what if suffering isn't God's doing at all? What if God didn't 'take' my husband or baby, didn't 'send' my cancer, or accident, or chronic pain? What if God never actively wills our suffering? What if God is as averse to human suffering as we are ourselves?

"This more positive image of God is, in fact, closer to revealed truth, and so discounts the above explanations for suffering. Yet even so, the question remains."

The question is a plaguing one, causing some, as Krisher also points out, to claim that suffering is sent as a punishment. Yet Jesus specifically refutes this in several different conversations with his followers. In one case when the disciples want to command fire to come from heaven and punish a Samaritan community that rejected Jesus, he strongly rebukes them and simply travels on to the next village. In another situation, Jesus takes the initiative, asking his followers if they believe that some men who were tortured and others who were killed in an accident had suffered these fates because they were sinners. Before anyone can reply, Jesus answers his own question, telling them that these victims were no worse sinners than others, but that all should view their suffering as a sign and opportunity to repent.

In the well-known—and rather surprising, especially for the people of those times—parable of the Prodigal Son, we hear Jesus telling of a reprobate son who, by all accounts, should have been severely punished or even banished by his father but was instead welcomed and celebrated. Jesus presents this father's forgiveness as a right and just outcome, offering it as an example of how the Father will act toward us.

Finally, in one of the most dramatic healings of his life—in no small way because it drew the ire of the religious and political leaders and probably gave his enemies the necessary ammunition to accuse him—Jesus restores sight to a blind man who was blind from birth. Before doing so, his apostles, having seen the man, ask Jesus whether this blindness is a result of the man's own sin or the sin of his parents. Jesus takes this opportunity not only to refute the idea that God sends such maladies as a form of punishment, but to further discredit the widely-held belief at the time that God punishes the children of sinful parents by plaguing those children with illness, disability, or any number of other tragic circumstances. After denying that either situation is the case, Jesus goes on to declare that this man's disease—and, we are able to presume, all dis-ease—may be seen as an chance to glorify God and demonstrate faith. Then, of course, Jesus heals the man.

Is this then the only real answer to why people suffer? So that we may have opportunities to glorify God? Could Jesus, God, be telling us that it is how we choose to respond to tragedy and illness that reflects our relationship with God? Should the real question be, not why does God allow suffering, but why do we respond to suffering by blaming God when we have been given the perfect opportunity to seek God?

Several years ago I facilitated a book group in my parish. Though the books we chose were not necessarily religious in nature, we often found our discussions centering on the spiritual. At one meeting we were discussing various religious practices when a new member asked plaintively, "Why do you Catholics have so many crosses in your churches?" We looked at her blankly. She continued, seeming almost offended, "I mean, you have all these crosses, and Jesus is usually stretched out in agony. Why don't you celebrate his life and resurrection instead of his death?" When she was finished, everyone looked at me.

Like I had the answer??

I was more stymied by the strong feelings that came through in her voice, the sense that she really didn't understand and was truly distressed by what she saw as misdirected energy, if not misdirected worship. But I understood what she meant. Every year we spend three days marking Jesus's suffering and death and only one hour on Sunday morning rejoicing in the Easter miracle. And to a stranger entering a Catholic church, the sight of at least one, and often more, depictions of Jesus writhing on the cross could certainly suggest a morbid sort of religion.

I can't remember what I told that woman, and when I think about it now, I still understand her confusion. Yet I might have a better answer today. Yes, the cross represents for us all of the sins we've committed and that Jesus had to die for. Still, there's something more. I think we focus on the cross because it is the one tangible sign that God is with us in our suffering. There is nothing, in terms of sorrow or pain or betrayal or temptation, we can experience that Jesus did not. Nothing proves this so much as a symbol of his suffering on the cross. The cross, then, becomes the answer to that question we should ask when we suffer: how do we respond to our suffering? The cross and all it represents presents us with the perfect invitation to seek God from the center of our own pain. Because he's already there.

And I've come to believe there's a "second" bottom line underscoring the question of suffering and God. It is unnervingly simple: we cannot know God, and therefore, we cannot know why God allows suffering, anymore than we can know why God allows joy or why he allows snakes or why he allows kittens. This is not the answer anyone wants to hear; I recoiled from it myself at first. We want someone to assure us that God is so loving, so in love with us, that he simply could not have any role in our suffering. We want to be told that God, in fact, has nothing to do with human suffering. Yet the fact is, we cannot know; we cannot fathom God.

When we perceive an event as irredeemably wrong or unjust—such as September 11, 2001, or horrifying natural disasters—we perceive on a very limited basis. We cannot imagine how much more width and depth and height has God's perception. When we see something as not possibly fitting in to a loving God's plan, we see it as humans see, with all our petty needs and carefully defined loves. We cannot see as God sees. Indeed, as we know from the relationship between Moses and God, the Lord does not reveal even the smallest bit of his true Being, lest the intensity of that experience instantly destroy us. If we cannot survive even a fraction of a glimpse of God, how can we possibly expect to know his plan or his definition of love?

It is in human nature to want to know, and thus lay claim to, some part of the Creator. Possibly this is our greatest arrogance. Because wanting to understand and explain the Creator is different from desiring the Creator. Yearning to be part of God and privy to God's plan is different from yearning for God. The former pursuit is the pursuit of a child who wants to share the parent's control; the latter is that of the child for whom the parent is all.

There is one certainty about God that we, even with minds constrained by humanity, can embrace: God, in everything, is our loving Creator Witness. He witnesses all that we experience, and all that we never will experience. The Lord sees a "big picture" that is so massive, we cannot even imagine it. But God is no engineer gazing dispassionately upon an invention. The loving Creator Witness is just that: our maker witnessing us with incomprehensible love and compassion. Witnessing our pain, even when it comes in strike after strike. Witnessing our joy, even when it is spare. Witnessing every event in our small, short histories, from the smallest habit to the life-changing event. Witnessing as one who lovingly stands by us and does not blink or turn away, ever.

In the end, this is all we can ask, all we should ask, and the only answer we can absolutely rely on. Beyond this is only trust.

Peter, finally, came to embrace this trust. What he comes to understand is a truth we must all strive to embrace as we go forward: as God's works-in-progress, we can only succeed by giving ourselves over to the shaping of our loving Creator Witness. In that effort, we may learn to see our repeated adversities as repeated opportunities to yield and yearn toward God. At times, it will be extremely difficult, even grueling: just look at what Peter went through. Then look at what he became. With God, for every second (third, fourth, or seventh times seventieth) strike, there is a corresponding new chance. Take it.

TALKING IT OVER WITH GOD

Lord, I now put myself in your hands knowing that you will be shaping and transforming me throughout my life. There are no guarantees in the lives of we humans. I know that. This sorrow and trouble may return to my life, in this form or another. Likewise, joy and peace may enfold me. Probably both will happen. But I will not be the one to say when or how or why. I now understand that I don't have that power— much as I may want it! I don't have the control I crave; nor will I ever have it.

It is true: you are the Potter and I am the clay. I won't pretend that I'm not afraid, Lord. You know I am. Yet I accept my fear with my faith, knowing that you will shape me as I need to be shaped. I know that you will stay with me through everything, Lord; I only ask that you allow me to always feel the warmth, grace and comfort of your presence.

ASK YOURSELF

1. If you are the clay and God the sculptor, at what stage would you now be: a lump of clay, a partly-formed creation, a nearly finished product with flaws yet to be smoothed over?

2. Can you identify any incident or moment in your life which God has started to shape you?

3. Have you ever resisted God's shaping hand in your life?

TAKING FURTHER ACTION

• Read Tom Cowan's *The Way of the Saints*, concentrating on those individuals who, in the midst of extreme adversity, offered themselves to God to be shaped into saints.

• Read the Gospel of John from chapter 13 to the end, paying careful attention to Peter's repeated troubles and taking heart in his wondrous redemption.

Search the New Testament for stories about Peter. Look particularly for Scripture passages that recount Peter committing some blunder. There are many examples: he doesn't want Jesus to let Levi (Matthew) join the disciples because Levi is a tax collector; he impulsively jumps out of the boat to meet Jesus walking on the sea in a raging storm, and then loses his faith and falters; after Jesus is transfigured and appears with Moses and Elijah, he tells Jesus they should construct three tents and stay on the mountain forever; he reprimands Jesus for insisting on speaking of the coming crucifixion; he refuses to let Jesus wash his face. And let's not forget the biggie: he promises to die for Jesus, and within twelve hours, denies him not once, but three times!

Select two of the "Peter" stories and compare them with your own mistakes. Depending upon which stories you select, you might think of times you've stereotyped and rejected a stranger, times you've been impulsive and then faded in the stretch, times you've spoken out of turn or out of ignorance. Repent those "Peter-esque" moments. And then read the end of the story, understanding that, like Peter, you too can become God's work-in-progress—if only you recognize the opportunity.